Mapping
The World

✳ ✳ ✳

Mapping
The World

A Mapping and Coloring Book of World History

VOLUME TWO: *since* 1300

BONNIE G. SMITH
MARC VAN DE MIEROOP
RICHARD VON GLAHN
KRIS LANE

New York   Oxford
OXFORD UNIVERSITY PRESS

Oxford University Press is a department of the University of Oxford.
It furthers the University's objective of excellence in research,
scholarship, and education by publishing worldwide.
Oxford is a registered trade mark of Oxford University Press
in the UK and certain other countries.

Published in the United States of America by Oxford University Press
198 Madison Avenue, New York, NY 10016, United States of America.

For titles covered by Section 112 of the US Higher Education
Opportunity Act, please visit www.oup.com/us/he for the latest
information about pricing and alternate formats.

Library of Congress Cataloging-in-Publication Data

Names: Smith, Bonnie G., 1940- author. | Van de Mieroop, Marc,
    author. | Von Glahn, Richard, author. | Lane, Kris E., 1967- author.
Title: Mapping the world : a mapping and coloring book of world
    history / Bonnie G. Smith, Marc Van De Mieroop, Richard von
    Glahn, Kris Lane.
Description: First edition. | New York, New York : Oxford University
    Press, 2019- | Includes index.
Identifiers: LCCN 2018033053 (print) | LCCN 2018046847 (ebook) |
    ISBN 9780190941192 (eBook) | ISBN 99780190941208 (eBook) |
    ISBN 9780190922412 (pbk. - v. 1) | ISBN 9780190922429 (pbk. - v. 2)
Subjects: LCSH: World history. | World history--Pictorial works. |
    World history--Maps. | Historical geography.
Classification: LCC D21 (ebook) | LCC D21 .S624 2019 (print) |
    DDC 911--dc23 LC record available at
    https://lccn.loc.gov/2018033053

9 8 7 6 5 4 3
Printed by LSC Communications, United States of America

Table of Contents

Introduction

THERE ARE MANY WAYS TO TELL A STORY. Textbooks offer narratives, crafted by a historian or a team of historians. Collections of primary sources present a mosaic of stories, often interspersed with pictures of artwork and other physical objects drawn from the past. *Mapping the World* takes advantage of the strength of maps to tell a different sort of story. Maps can reveal connections by tracing networks—of trade, migration, and cultural exchange. Maps can also act as snapshots of social history, conveying in dramatic visual terms developments related to demographic and economic growth or change. Like networks, such social trends often do not show clearly in political narratives or literary sources. Finally, maps are an excellent medium for conveying the transregional and even global nature of many deep processes, from migration patterns to industrialization to climate change.

Maps use a unique visual language to convey a great deal of information in simple form. The maps in this atlas use a variety of different projections—a technique used to show the Earth's curved surface on a flat plane—to trace the geographical, physical, and social development of humans from over 1 million years ago to the present. The maps also include keys, or legends, that explain the symbols used on each map. Many of the maps also show topography or relief—the contours of the land. Topography is an important element in studying maps because the physical terrain has played a critical role in shaping human history.

The maps are divided into two groups: (a) reference maps that provide a brief outline of key events and developments in global history and (b) blank outline maps and accompanying exercises that offer opportunities to explore the past in a hands-on fashion.

When working with the outline maps, use colored pencils or fine-point felt-tip pens. Do not use crayons.

The pages for the outline maps are perforated so they can be easily separated and turned in for grading.

An answer key for the outline maps is available to instructors. Please contact your local Oxford University Press representative for information on how to access the answer key.

Acknowledgements

Our heartfelt thanks to Charles Cavaliere, executive editor at Oxford University Press, for conceiving of this workbook. He astutely noted that the increasing popularity of coloring books among general readers offered an opportunity to provide students with a resource they could use to improve their geography skills We are also indebted to editorial assistants Rowan Wixted and Katie Tunkavige for organizing our files. Matthew Fox, production manager, kept everyone on task and devised creative workarounds to last-minute obstacles that we faced. Thanks to everyone's hard work, we can now sharpen our coloring pencils. We hope you do the same.

Reference Maps

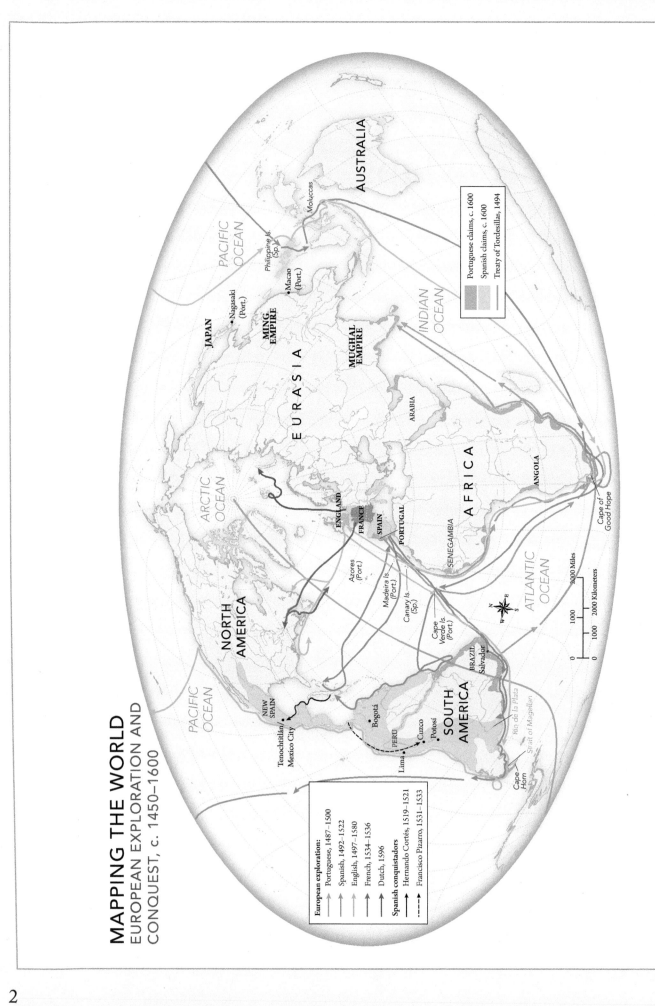

MAPPING THE WORLD
EUROPEAN EXPLORATION AND CONQUEST, c. 1450–1600

European exploration:
↑ Portuguese, 1487–1500
↑ Spanish, 1492–1522
↑ English, 1497–1580
↑ French, 1534–1536
↑ Dutch, 1596

Spanish conquistadors
→ Hernando Cortés, 1519–1521
→ Francisco Pizarro, 1531–1533

Portuguese claims, c. 1600
Spanish claims, c. 1600
Treaty of Tordesillas, 1494

PACIFIC OCEAN

AUSTRALIA

Moluccas

Philippine Is. (Sp.)

Macao (Port.)

Nagasaki (Port.)

JAPAN

MING EMPIRE

EURASIA

MUGHAL EMPIRE

INDIAN OCEAN

ARABIA

AFRICA

ANGOLA

SENEGAMBIA

Cape of Good Hope

ARCTIC OCEAN

ENGLAND
FRANCE
SPAIN
PORTUGAL

Azores (Port.)

Madeira Is. (Port.)

Canary Is. (Sp.)

Cape Verde Is. (Port.)

ATLANTIC OCEAN

NORTH AMERICA

PACIFIC OCEAN

NEW SPAIN

Tenochtitlán/ Mexico City

Bogotá

PERU

Lima

Cuzco

Potosí

SOUTH AMERICA

Río de la Plata

BRAZIL
Salvador

Strait of Magellan

Cape Horn

3000 Miles

0   1000   2000 Kilometers
0   1000   2000

N
W   E
S

Mapping The World
European Exploration and Conquest, c. 1450–1600

Combining a variety of shipbuilding and navigating technologies in innovative ways and arming themselves with powerful new guns, western Europeans set out in search of spices, gold, and slaves. Some also sought Christian allies and converts. Merchants shared knowledge and pooled capital in Portugal's capital of Lisbon, the first seat of truly global maritime exploration. Soon after the Portuguese came the Spanish, among them settlers, traders, missionaries, and—most famously—conquistadors. These toppled the great American empires of the Aztecs and Incas within a generation of Columbus's landing in the Caribbean. The French, Dutch, and English followed the Iberian lead, but had little to show for their efforts before 1600.

Timeline

- **1441** First sub-Saharan Africans captured and taken by ship to Portugal
- **1492** Fall of Granada and expulsion of Jews in Spain; Columbus reaches America
- **1494** Treaty of Tordesillas divides known world between Portugal and Spain
- **1498** Vasco da Gama becomes first European to reach India by sea
- **1500** Portuguese reach Brazil
- **1519–1521** Spanish conquest of Aztec Mexico
- **1519–1522** Magellan's ship circumnavigates the globe
- **1532–1536** Spanish conquest of Inca Peru
- **1545** Discovery of silver deposits at Potosí
- **1549** Portuguese establish royal capital of Salvador; first Jesuits arrive in Brazil
- **1555** French establish colony in Brazil's Guanabara Bay
- **1564** Discovery of mercury mines in Huancavelica, Peru
- **1567** Portuguese drive French from Brazil
- **1572** Mita labor draft and mercury amalgamation formalized in Brazil
- **1570–1571** Inquisition established in Lima and Mexico City
- **1592** Potosí reaches peak production
- **1599** Great Mapuche uprising in Chile

MAPPING THE WORLD
AFRICA AND THE ATLANTIC, c. 1450–1800

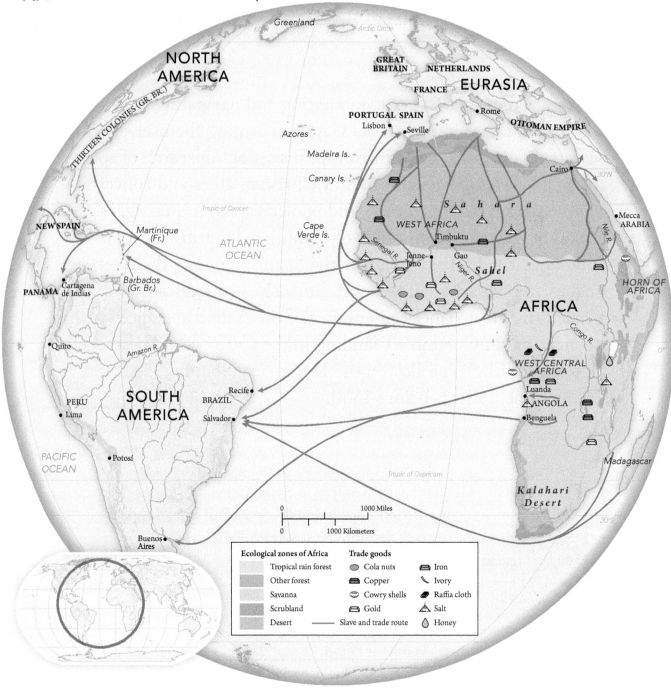

Greenland

NORTH AMERICA

Arctic Circle

GREAT BRITAIN
NETHERLANDS
FRANCE
EURASIA

THIRTEEN COLONIES (GR. BR.)

PORTUGAL SPAIN
Lisbon
Seville
Rome
OTTOMAN EMPIRE

Azores

Madeira Is.

Canary Is.

Cairo

30°N

NEW SPAIN

Martinique
(Fr.)

Tropic of Cancer

Cape Verde Is.

ATLANTIC OCEAN

S a h a r a

WEST AFRICA

Timbuktu

Mecca
ARABIA

Nile R.

PANAMA
Cartagena
de Indias

Barbados
(Gr. Br.)

Senegal R.

Jenne-
Jeno

Gao

Niger R.

S a h e l

HORN OF AFRICA

AFRICA

Quito

Amazon R.

Congo R.

0°

PERU
Lima

SOUTH AMERICA

BRAZIL

Recife

Salvador

WEST CENTRAL AFRICA

Luanda
ANGOLA

Benguela

PACIFIC OCEAN

Potosí

Tropic of Capricorn

Madagascar

30°S

Kalahari Desert

Buenos
Aires

0   1000 Miles

0   1000 Kilometers

Ecological zones of Africa

Tropical rain forest

Other forest

Savanna

Scrubland

Desert

Trade goods

Cola nuts

Copper

Cowry shells

Gold

Slave and trade route

Iron

Ivory

Raffia cloth

Salt

Honey

Mapping The World
Africa and the Atlantic, c. 1450–1800

The vast and ecologically diverse continent of Africa had long been linked together by trade in salt, copper, iron, cola nuts, and other commodities. It had also been connected since ancient times to the Mediterranean and the Indian Ocean maritime worlds. Goods traded beyond Africa consisted mostly of gold and ivory, but there was also substantial traffic in human captives. After 1450, the Portuguese extended this pattern into the growing Atlantic world, establishing fortified trading posts all along Africa's west coast.

Timeline

- **c. 1100–1500** Extended dry period in West Africa prompts migrations
- **c. 1450** Kingdom of Benin reaches height of its power
- **c. 1464–1492** Reign of Sunni Ali in the Songhai Empire
- **1482** Portuguese establish trading fort of São Jorge da Mina (Ghana)
- **1506–1543** Reign of Alfonso I (Nzinga Mbemba) of kingdom of Kongo
- **1569** Collapse of kingdom of Kongo
- **1574** Portuguese-aided restoration of kingdom of Kongo
- **1591** Moroccan raiders conquer Songhal Empire
- **1621** Formation of Dutch West India Company
- **1624–1663** Reign of Queen Nzinga in the Ndongo kingdom of Angola
- **1638–1641** Dutch seize São Jorge da Mina and Luanda
- **1672** Formation of English Royal African Company
- **1750–1800** Atlantic slave trade reaches highest volume
- **1807** British declare Atlantic slave trade illegal

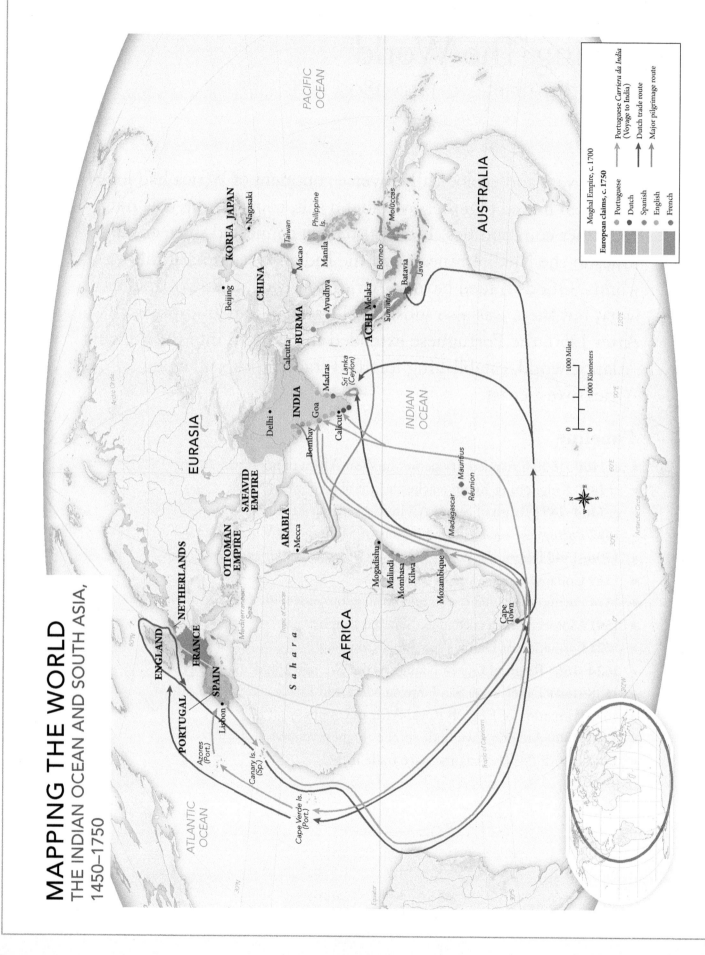

MAPPING THE WORLD
THE INDIAN OCEAN AND SOUTH ASIA, 1450–1750

Legend:

Mughal Empire, c. 1700

European claims, c. 1750

- Portuguese *Carriera da India* (Voyage to India)
- Dutch trade route
- Major pilgrimage route

Portuguese | Dutch | Spanish | English | French

Labels on map:

ATLANTIC OCEAN
PACIFIC OCEAN
INDIAN OCEAN

EURASIA
AFRICA
AUSTRALIA

ENGLAND
NETHERLANDS
FRANCE
SPAIN
PORTUGAL
Lisbon
Azores (Port.)
Canary Is. (Sp.)
Cape Verde Is. (Port.)

OTTOMAN EMPIRE
Mediterranean Sea
SAFAVID EMPIRE
ARABIA
Mecca
Sahara
Tropic of Cancer

Mogadishu
Malindi
Mombasa
Kilwa
Mozambique
Cape Town
Madagascar
Mauritius
Réunion

Tropic of Capricorn
Equator

INDIA
Delhi
Bombay
Goa
Calicut
Madras
Sri Lanka (Ceylon)
Calcutta
BURMA
Ayudhya
ACEH
Melaka
Sumatra
Java
Batavia
Borneo
Moluccas
Philippine Is.
Manila

CHINA
Beijing
Macao
Taiwan
KOREA
JAPAN
Nagasaki

N E S W

1000 Miles
1000 Kilometers

60N 30N 0° 30W
30E 60E 90E 120E

Arctic Circle
Antarctic Circle

Mapping The World
The Indian Ocean and South Asia, 1450–1750

Harnessing the power of monsoon winds, Arab and Asian sailors traversed the Indian Ocean and Arabian Sea for centuries before the Portuguese arrived in the 1490s in search of pepper and other commodities. In subsequent years, competing Eurasian interlopers, including the Ottomans, conquered key ports from East Africa to Southeast Asia in an attempt to control both exports to Europe and interregional trade. The Ottomans retreated after the mid-sixteenth century, but many Muslims continued to sail to the Arabian peninsula to make the pilgrimage to Mecca and to engage in trade.

Timeline

- **1336–1565** Vijayanagara kingdom in southern India
- **1498** Vasco da Gama reaches India
- **1500–1763** Mughal Empire in South Asia
- **1509–1529** Reign of Krishna Deva Raya of Vijayanagara
- **1510** Portuguese conquest of Goa, India
- **1511** Portuguese conquest of Melaka
- **1517** Portuguese establish fort in Sri Lanka (Ceylon)
- **1526** Battle of Panipat led by Mughal emperor Babur
- **1530** Consolidation of Aceh under sultan Ali Mughayat Syah
- **1556–1605** Reign of Mughal emperor Akbar
- **1567** Akbar's siege of Chitor
- **1600** English East India Company founded in London
- **1602** Atlantic slave trade reaches highest volume
- **1605–1627** Dutch East India Company (VOC) founded in Amsterdam
- **1641** Dutch take Melaka from Portuguese
- **1641–1699** Sultanate of Women in Aceh
- **1658** Dutch drive Portuguese from Ceylon
- **1701** William Kidd hanged in London for piracy
- **1739** Persian raiders under Nadir Shah sack Delhi
- **1764** British East India Company controls Bengal

MAPPING THE WORLD
EUROPE AND THE GREATER MEDITERRANEAN, c. 1600

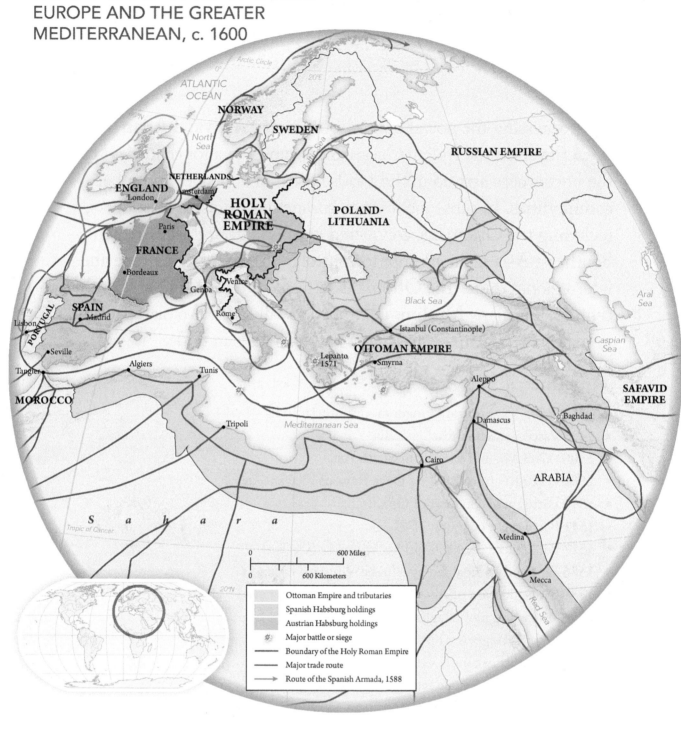

NORWAY

SWEDEN

RUSSIAN EMPIRE

ATLANTIC
OCEAN

Arctic Circle

North
Sea

NETHERLANDS

ENGLAND
Amsterdam

London

HOLY
ROMAN
EMPIRE

POLAND-
LITHUANIA

Paris

FRANCE

Bordeaux

Venice

Genoa

SPAIN

Rome

Black Sea

Aral
Sea

PORTUGAL

Madrid

Lisbon

Istanbul (Constantinople)

Caspian
Sea

Seville

OTTOMAN EMPIRE

Lepanto
1571

Smyrna

Tangier

Algiers

Tunis

Aleppo

SAFAVID
EMPIRE

MOROCCO

Damascus

Baghdad

Tripoli

Mediterranean Sea

Cairo

ARABIA

S a h a r a

Tropic of Cancer

Medina

20°N

Mecca

Red Sea

0   600 Miles

0   600 Kilometers

▨	Ottoman Empire and tributaries
▨	Spanish Habsburg holdings
▨	Austrian Habsburg holdings
✹	Major battle or siege
——	Boundary of the Holy Roman Empire
——	Major trade route
→	Route of the Spanish Armada, 1588

Mapping The World
Europe and the Greater Mediterranean, c. 1600

The Mediterranean was an ancient global crossroads, and its role in connecting Africa, Asia, and Europe only intensified during early modern times. After 1450, African gold and Spanish American silver lubricated trade, but they also financed warfare, notably an increasingly bitter rivalry between the Ottoman and Habsburg Empires. The period also witnessed the rise of the so-called Barbary pirates, based mostly in Algiers, Tunis, and Tripoli, who offered only a tenuous allegiance to the Ottomans against their Christian foes. Mediterranean trade, sea routes to the Indian Ocean, and overland routes to East Asia were all increasingly tied to Europe's North Atlantic trade. As trade grew, conflict became ever more intense.

Timeline

- **1453** Ottoman conquest of Constantinople
- **1492** Spanish take Granada, expel Jews
- **1517** Martin Luther disseminates Ninety-Five Theses, sparking the Protestant Reformation
- **1520–1566** Reign of Ottoman emperor Suleiman
- **1540** Ignatius Loyola founds the new Catholic order of the Jesuits
- **1543** Nicolaus Copernicus, *On the Revolutions of the Heavenly Spheres*
- **1545–1563** Council of Trent
- **1571** Battle of Lepanto
- **1572** St. Bartholomew's Day massacre
- **1580** Philip II of Spain takes over Portuguese Empire
- **1598** Edict of Nantes ends French Religious War
- **1618–1648** Thirty Years' War
- **1640** Portugal wins independence from Spain
- **1642–1646** English Civil War
- **1643–1715** Reign of Louis XIV of France
- **1683** Ottomans defeated in Vienna by Polish–Austrian alliance
- **1687** Isaac Newton, *Principia Mathematica*
- **1688** Glorious Revolution in England
- **1701–1714** War of the Spanish Succession

MAPPING THE WORLD
EURASIAN TRADE AND EMPIRES, c. 1700

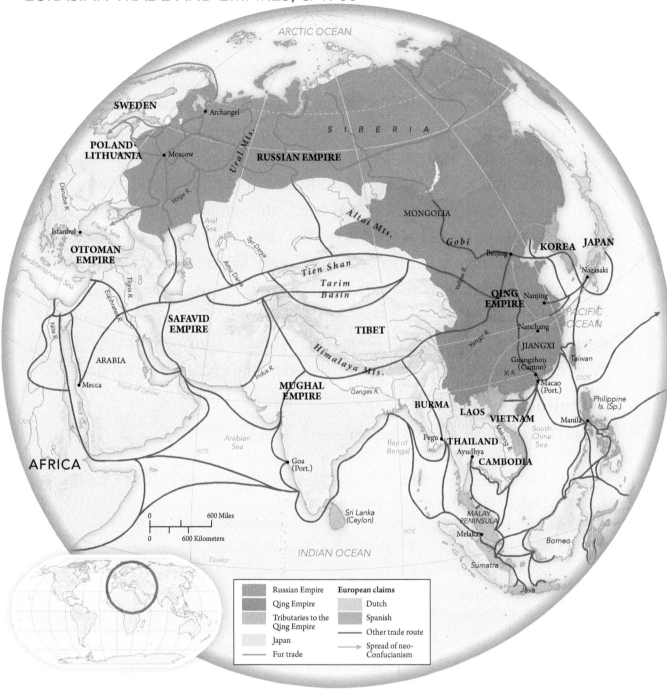

ARCTIC OCEAN

SWEDEN
• Archangel

SIBERIA

POLAND-
LITHUANIA
• Moscow
Ural Mts.
RUSSIAN EMPIRE

Danube R.
Volga R.
Aral Sea
Altai Mts.
MONGOLIA
Gobi

Istanbul •
Black Sea
KOREA JAPAN
• Beijing
Nagasaki

OTTOMAN
EMPIRE
Mediterranean Sea
Caspian Sea
Syr Darya
Tien Shan
Tarim Basin
QING
EMPIRE Nanjing
PACIFIC OCEAN

Tigris R.
Euphrates R.
Amu Darya
Nanchang

Nile R.
SAFAVID
EMPIRE
TIBET
Yangzi R.
JIANGXI

ARABIA
Himalaya Mts.
Indus R.
Guangzhou
(Canton)
Xi R.
Taiwan

Mecca •
Tropic of Cancer
MUGHAL
EMPIRE
Ganges R.
Macao
(Port.)
Philippine
Is. (Sp.)

BURMA
LAOS VIETNAM
South
China
Sea
Manila

Arabian
Sea
Bay of
Bengal
Pegu •
THAILAND
Ayudhya
Mekong R.
CAMBODIA

AFRICA
Red Sea
Goa
(Port.)

Sri Lanka
(Ceylon)
MALAY
PENINSULA
Melaka
Borneo

0   600 Miles

0   600 Kilometers
Equator
INDIAN OCEAN
Sumatra
Java

	Russian Empire	European claims	
	Qing Empire		Dutch
	Tributaries to the Qing Empire		Spanish
	Japan		Other trade route
	Fur trade		Spread of neo-Confucianism

Mapping The World
Eurasian Trade and Empires, c. 1700

With the decline of the Mongols, central Asia returned to its former role as a trading crossroads, mostly for silk, gems, furs, and other high-value commodities, yet it also became a meeting ground for two new, expansive empires: Russia under the Romanovs and China under the Qing, or Manchu, dynasty. Despite their focus on land expansion, both empires sought trade ties with the outside world by sea, mostly to win foreign exchange in the form of silver. More isolated areas in the region included Korea and Japan, both of which experienced political consolidation influenced by the spread of Chinese neo-Confucianist principles. Similar processes appeared in Vietnam, whereas most of mainland Southeast Asia remained under expansionist Buddhist kings.

Timeline

- **1392–1910** Yi dynasty established in Korea
- **1542** Jesuits reach Japan
- **1555–1581** Expansion of Burma under King Bayinnaung
- **1565** Spanish conquest of Philippines begins
- **1571** Manila becomes Philippine capital and key Pacific trading post
- **1581** Chinese Ming emperor Wanli issues Single Whip Law
- **1584–1613** Times of Troubles in Russia
- **1597–1630s** Persecution of Japanese Christians
- **1601** Matteo Ricci demonstrates Western technology in Ming court
- **1602–1867** Tokugawa shogunate in Japan
- **1614** Japanese contact with foreigners restricted
- **1627, 1636** Manchu invasion of Korea
- **1644** Manchu invasion of Beijing; Ming dynasty replaced by Qing
- **1661–1722** Quin expansion under Emperor Kangxi
- **1689–1725** Russian imperial expansion under Tsar Peter the Great
- **1751** Qing annexation of Tibet

MAPPING THE WORLD
NEW WORLD COLONIES, c. 1750

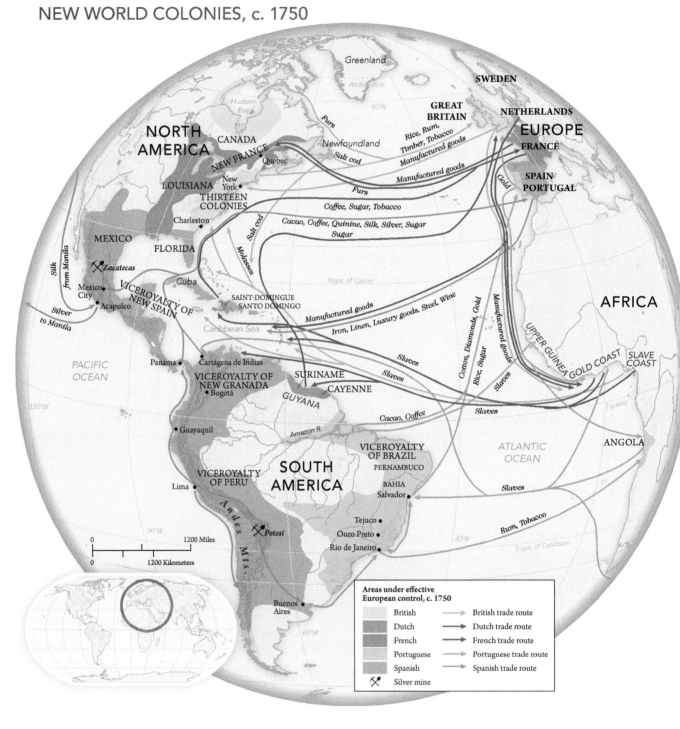

Greenland

Arctic Circle

SWEDEN

60°N

GREAT BRITAIN

NETHERLANDS

EUROPE

FRANCE

SPAIN
PORTUGAL

Hudson Bay

NORTH AMERICA

CANADA

NEW FRANCE

Furs

Newfoundland

Salt cod

Quebec

Rice, Rum, Timber, Tobacco

Manufactured goods

Manufactured goods

Gold

30°N

LOUISIANA

New York

THIRTEEN COLONIES

Furs

Coffee, Sugar, Tobacco

Charleston

Salt cod

Cacao, Coffee, Quinine, Silk, Silver, Sugar

Sugar

MEXICO

FLORIDA

Molasses

Silk from Manila

Zacatecas

Cuba

Tropic of Cancer

AFRICA

Mexico City

VICEROYALTY OF NEW SPAIN

Acapulco

SAINT-DOMINGUE
SANTO DOMINGO

Manufactured goods

Silver to Manila

Caribbean Sea

Iron, Linen, Luxury goods, Steel, Wine

Cotton, Diamonds, Gold

Manufactured goods

UPPER GUINEA

GOLD COAST

SLAVE COAST

PACIFIC OCEAN

Panama

Cartagena de Indias

VICEROYALTY OF NEW GRANADA

Bogotá

SURINAME

CAYENNE

GUYANA

Slaves

Slaves

Rice, Sugar

Slaves

Equator

120°W

Guayaquil

Amazon R.

Cacao, Coffee

Slaves

ATLANTIC OCEAN

ANGOLA

VICEROYALTY OF BRAZIL

PERNAMBUCO

SOUTH AMERICA

Lima

VICEROYALTY OF PERU

BAHIA

Salvador

Slaves

0°

Andes Mts.

Tejuco

Ouro Preto

Potosí

Rio de Janeiro

Rum, Tobacco

90°W

30°W

Tropic of Capricorn

0   1200 Miles

0   1200 Kilometers

Buenos Aires

60°W

Areas under effective European control, c. 1750

British	→ British trade route
Dutch	→ Dutch trade route
French	→ French trade route
Portuguese	→ Portuguese trade route
Spanish	→ Spanish trade route
✗ Silver mine	

Mapping The World
New World Colonies, c. 1750

Arguably the most profoundly transformed world region in the early modern period, the Americas soon came to be linked not only to western Europe, but also to Atlantic Africa and East Asia. Native American populations declined drastically as a result of disease and conquest. Their numbers began to rebound after 1650, however, and in Spanish America they served as the major producers of silver, dyes, hides, and other commodities exported to the rest of the world. Africa's role was also critical. The number of enslaved Africans forcibly brought to the Americas by 1750 far exceeded the number of Europeans who migrated voluntarily, they and their descendants produced the bulk of the world's sugar, cacao, tobacco, and eventually coffee. Colonial American life entailed more than forced labor and primary resource extraction, but both, like the Christianity introduced by missionaries and colonists, remained core features of the region long after colonialism ended.

Timeline

- **1570** Spanish galleons begin annual service linking Acapulco to Manila
- **1607** English establish colony at Jamestown, Virginia
- **1608** French establish colony at Quebec City
- **1618** Dutch establish colony of New Netherland on upper Hudson River
- **1625** Dutch settle New Amsterdam on Manhattan Island; English establish colony on Barbados
- **1630** Dutch capture northeast Brazil
- **1654** Portuguese drive Dutch from Brazil; some colonists move to Suriname
- **1655** English seize Jamaica from the Spanish
- **1664** English take New Amsterdam from Dutch, rename it New York
- **1671** Henry Morgan's buccaneers sack Panama City
- **1676** Bacon's Rebellion in Virginia
- **1694** Great Brazilian maroon community of Palmares destroyed
- **1695–1800** Discovery in Brazilian interior of gold and diamonds inaugurates Brazil's "gold rush"
- **1701–1714** War of the Spanish Succession
- **1720** Brazil elevated to status of viceroyalty
- **1763** Rio de Janeiro elevated to status of capital of Brazil

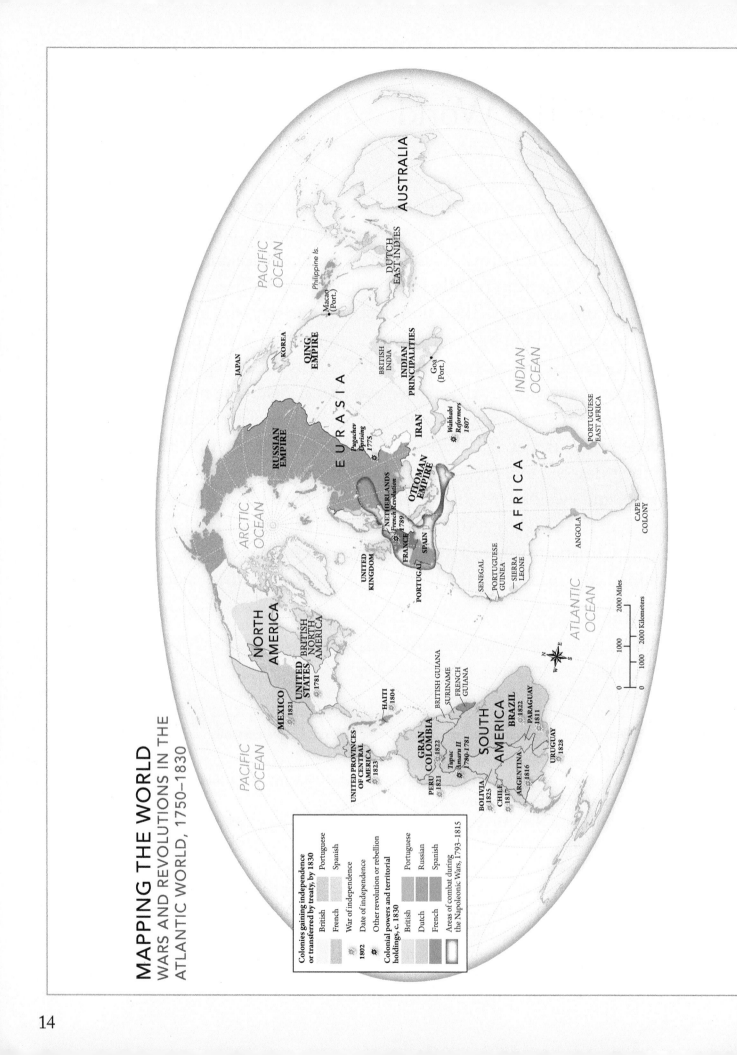

MAPPING THE WORLD
WARS AND REVOLUTIONS IN THE ATLANTIC WORLD, 1750–1830

Colonies gaining independence or transferred by treaty, by 1830

- British
- French
- Portuguese
- Spanish

- 🏵 War of independence
- **1802** Date of independence
- ✳ Other revolution or rebellion

Colonial powers and territorial holdings, c. 1830

- British
- Dutch
- French
- Portuguese
- Russian
- Spanish

- Areas of combat during the Napoleonic Wars, 1793–1815

PACIFIC OCEAN

ARCTIC OCEAN

AUSTRALIA

Philippine Is.

Macao (Port.)

DUTCH EAST INDIES

KOREA

JAPAN

QING EMPIRE

EURASIA

RUSSIAN EMPIRE

Pugachev Uprising 1775 ✳

BRITISH INDIA

INDIAN PRINCIPALITIES

Goa (Port.)

INDIAN OCEAN

IRAN

Wahhabi Reformers 1807 ✳

OTTOMAN EMPIRE

NETHERLANDS

French Revolution 1789 ✳

FRANCE

SPAIN

UNITED KINGDOM

PORTUGAL

AFRICA

SENEGAL

PORTUGUESE GUINEA

SIERRA LEONE

ANGOLA

PORTUGUESE EAST AFRICA

CAPE COLONY

NORTH AMERICA

BRITISH NORTH AMERICA

MEXICO 🏵 1821

UNITED STATES 🏵 1781

HAITI 🏵 1804

UNITED PROVINCES OF CENTRAL AMERICA 🏵 1823

BRITISH GUIANA

SURINAME

FRENCH GUIANA

GRAN COLOMBIA 🏵 1822

PERU 🏵 1821

Tupac Amaru II 1780–1781 ✳

BOLIVIA 🏵 1825

CHILE 🏵 1817

ARGENTINA 🏵 1816

SOUTH AMERICA

BRAZIL 🏵 1822

PARAGUAY 🏵 1811

URUGUAY 🏵 1828

ATLANTIC OCEAN

PACIFIC OCEAN

0   1000   2000 Miles
0   1000   2000 Kilometers

14

Mapping The World
Wars and Revolutions in the Atlantic World, 1750–1830

Between 1775 and 1830 transplanted Europeans, their descendants, and their slaves and servants overwhelmed the Spanish, British, and French Empires in the Western Hemisphere and created many independent nations. Europe and the Mediterranean also experienced revolutionary change as the ideas of just government and citizens' rights traveled the crossroads of the world and caused both transformation and turmoil.

Timeline

- **1751–1772** Publication of the *Encyclopedia*
- **1762** Jean-Jacques Rousseau publishes *The Social Contract* and *Emile*
- **1775–1781** Revolution in North America
- **1776** Adam Smith, *The Wealth of Nations*
- **1789** US Constitution formally adopted; revolution begins in France
- **1791** Revolution begins in Haiti
- **1792** France declared a republic; Mary Wollstonecraft writes *A Vindication of the Rights of Woman*
- **1799** Napoleon comes to power
- **1804** Haiti becomes independent from France
- **1811** Simon Bolivar first takes up arms against Spain
- **1815** Napoleon defeated at Waterloo; Congress of Vienna resettles the boundaries of European states
- **1816** Argentina becomes independent from Spain
- **1817** Chile becomes independent from Spain
- **1821** Mexico and Peru become independent from Spain
- **1822** Brazil becomes independent from Portugal
- **1825** Bolivia becomes independent from Spain

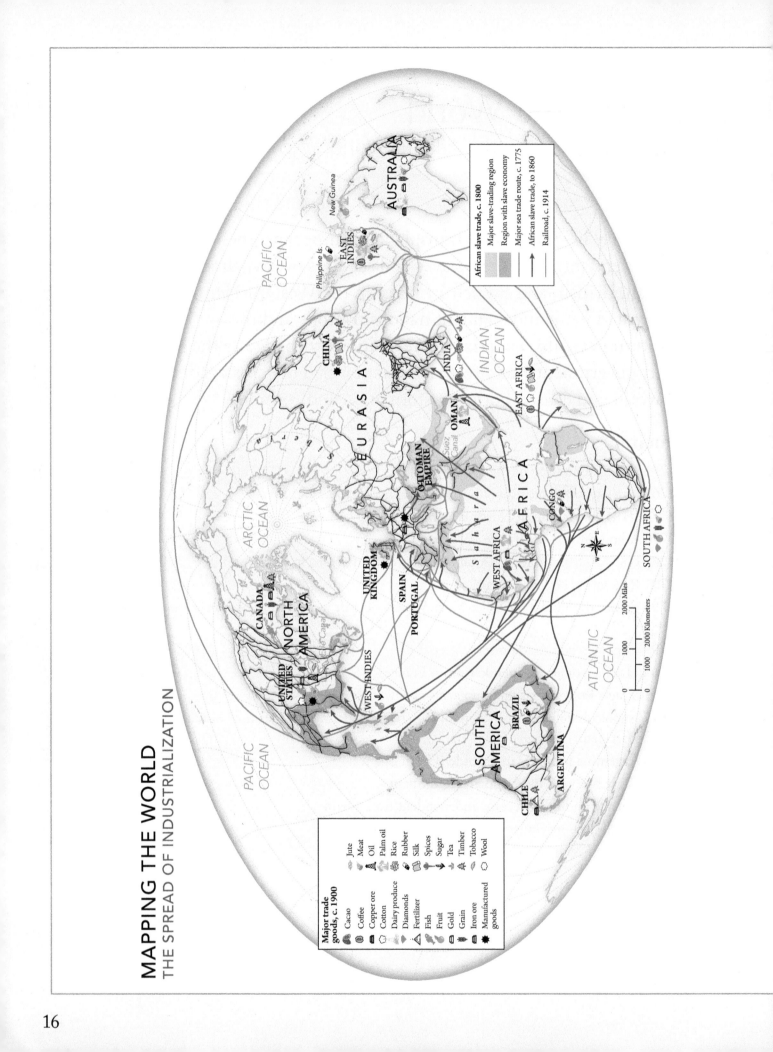

MAPPING THE WORLD
THE SPREAD OF INDUSTRIALIZATION

Major trade goods, c. 1900

Cacao		Jute	
Coffee		Meat	
Copper ore		Oil	
Cotton		Palm oil	
Dairy produce		Rice	
Diamonds		Rubber	
Fertilizer		Silk	
Fish		Spices	
Fruit		Sugar	
Gold		Tea	
Grain		Timber	
Iron ore		Tobacco	
Manufactured goods		Wool	

African slave trade, c. 1800

- Major slave-trading region
- Region with slave economy
- Major sea trade route, c. 1775
- African slave trade, to 1860
- Railroad, c. 1914

PACIFIC OCEAN

AUSTRALIA

New Guinea

EAST INDIES

Philippine Is.

CHINA

INDIA

INDIAN OCEAN

EAST AFRICA

EURASIA

Siberia

OMAN

Suez Canal

OTTOMAN EMPIRE

Sahara

AFRICA

WEST AFRICA

CONGO

SOUTH AFRICA

ARCTIC OCEAN

CANADA

NORTH AMERICA

UNITED KINGDOM

SPAIN

PORTUGAL

UNITED STATES

WEST INDIES

PACIFIC OCEAN

SOUTH AMERICA

BRAZIL

ARGENTINA

CHILE

ATLANTIC OCEAN

2000 Miles

2000 Kilometers

1000

1000

0

0

Mapping The World
The Spread of Industrialization

The world remained more agricultural than industrial in 1900. As the twentieth century opened, however, the Industrial Revolution that originated in eighteenth-century Britain was driving industry to ever-higher peaks. Among its globally significant consequences was the decline of the slave trade and slavery itself, which had previously greatly increased the world's productivity.

Timeline

- **c. 1750** Industrialization begins in Great Britain
- **1769** James Watt creates the modern steam engine
- **1780s–1790s** Interchangeability of parts developed in France
- **1803** Denmark becomes the first Western country to abolish the slave trade
- **1814** George Stephenson puts a steam engine on a carriage on rails, inventing the locomotive
- **1819** First Atlantic crossing by a steamship
- **1839–1842** Opium War between China and Britain
- **1840s–1864** Taiping Rebellion
- **1842** Treaty of Nanjing opens Chinese ports
- **1848** *Communist Manifesto* published
- **1853** US ships enter Japanese ports
- **1865** US Civil War ends, rapid US industrialization begins
- **1868** Meiji Restoration launches Japanese industrialization
- **1871** Germany gains resource-rich Alsace and Lorraine after defeating France
- **1873–c. 1900** Deep global recession with uneven recovery
- **1890s** Argentina's leading textile manufacturer produces 1.6 million yards of cloth annually
- **1891–1904** Construction of Trans-Siberian Railway

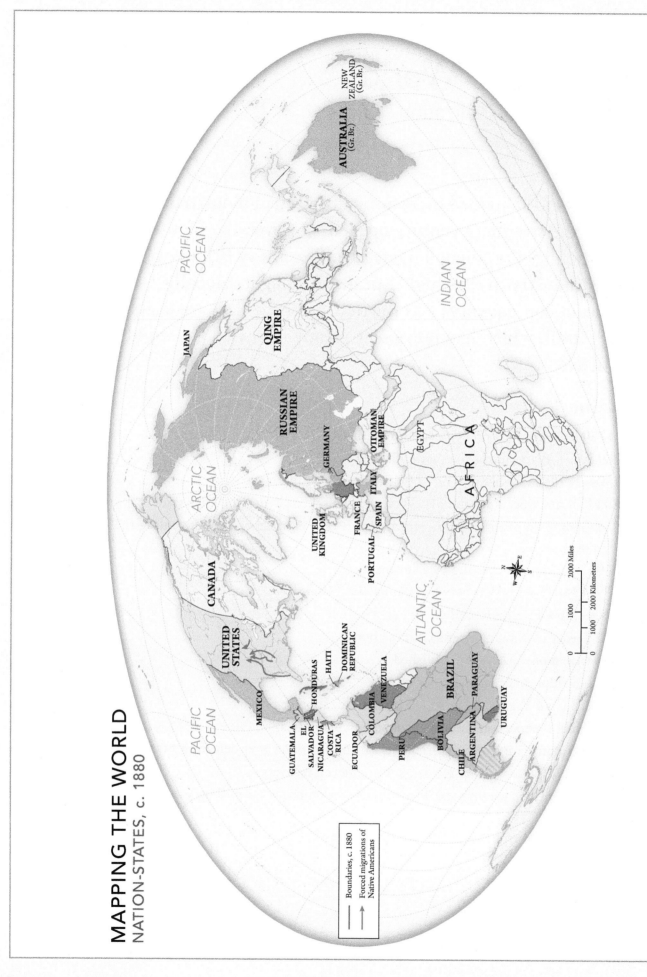

MAPPING THE WORLD
NATION-STATES, c. 1880

Boundaries, c. 1880

Forced migrations of
Native Americans

PACIFIC OCEAN

ARCTIC OCEAN

CANADA

UNITED STATES

MEXICO

GUATEMALA
EL SALVADOR
NICARAGUA
COSTA RICA
ECUADOR
HONDURAS
HAITI
DOMINICAN REPUBLIC
VENEZUELA
COLOMBIA
PERU
BOLIVIA
CHILE
ARGENTINA
BRAZIL
PARAGUAY
URUGUAY

ATLANTIC OCEAN

AUSTRALIA (Gr. Br.)

NEW ZEALAND (Gr. Br.)

QING EMPIRE

JAPAN

RUSSIAN EMPIRE

GERMANY

UNITED KINGDOM

FRANCE
PORTUGAL
SPAIN
ITALY
OTTOMAN EMPIRE

EGYPT

AFRICA

INDIAN OCEAN

PACIFIC OCEAN

N
E
S
W

0   1000   2000 Miles
0   1000   2000 Kilometers

Mapping The World
Nation-States, c. 1880

In many cases, but not all, industrial growth and revolutionary uprisings often led kingdoms to develop nation-states. Around the world, nations reformed their administrative structures, created more effective armies, and encouraged national spirit. From Russia to Australia and across the Western Hemisphere, war and the seizure of native peoples' lands accompanied the rise of the nation-state.

Timeline

- **1833–1855** Mexican caudillo Santa Anna serves at intervals to lead the government
- **1846–1848** Mexican–American War
- **1853–1856** Crimean War
- **1855** Walt Whitman, *Leaves of Grass*
- **1859–1870** Unification of Italy
- **1860s** Height of opera singer Angela Peralta's career
- **1861** Emancipation of the serfs in Russia
- **1861–1865** US Civil War
- **1863** Emancipation Proclamation in the United States
- **1866–1871** Unification of Germany
- **1868** Meiji Restoration of Japan
- **1865** US Civil War ends, rapid US industrialization begins
- **1868** Meiji Restoration launches Japanese industrialization
- **1872–1876** Fukuzawa Yukichi, *Encouragement of Learning*
- **1880s** Popular uprisings in Japan
- **1881** Young rebels assassinate Alexander II of Russia
- **1888** Emancipation of slaves in Brazil
- **1889** Brazilian emperor Pedro II abdicates and republic is installed

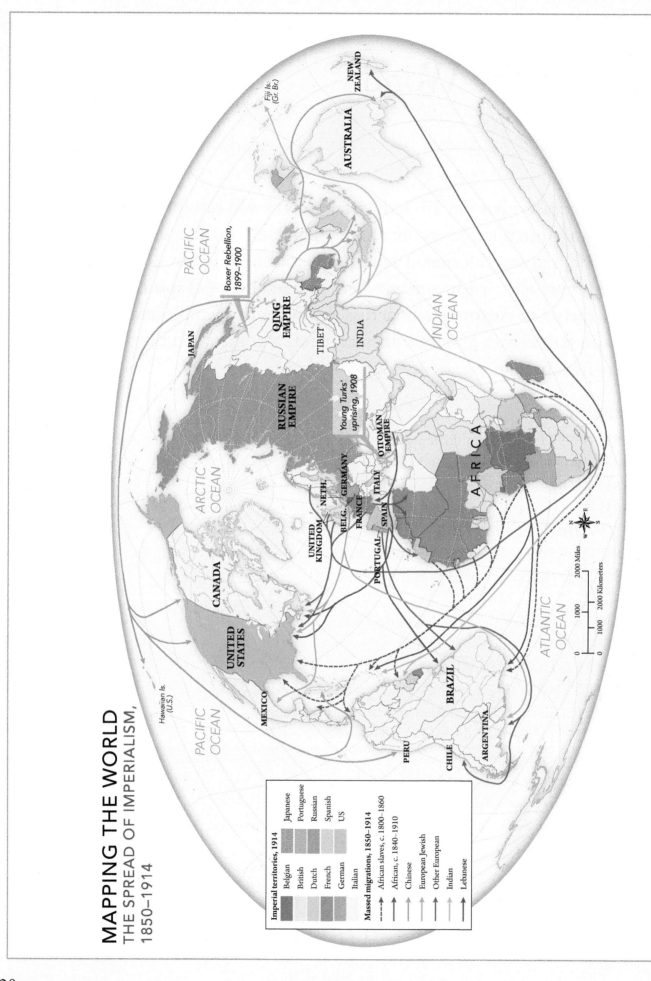

MAPPING THE WORLD
THE SPREAD OF IMPERIALISM, 1850–1914

Imperial territories, 1914

Belgian	Japanese
British	Portuguese
Dutch	Russian
French	Spanish
German	US
Italian	

Massed migrations, 1850–1914

African slaves, c. 1800–1860
African, c. 1840–1910
Chinese
European Jewish
Other European
Indian
Lebanese

Boxer Rebellion, 1899–1900

Young Turks' uprising, 1908

PACIFIC OCEAN

NEW ZEALAND

AUSTRALIA

Fiji Is. (Gr. Br.)

QING EMPIRE

JAPAN

TIBET

INDIA

INDIAN OCEAN

RUSSIAN EMPIRE

ARCTIC OCEAN

AFRICA

OTTOMAN EMPIRE

GERMANY

NETH.

BELG.

FRANCE

ITALY

SPAIN

PORTUGAL

UNITED KINGDOM

CANADA

UNITED STATES

MEXICO

Hawaiian Is. (U.S.)

PACIFIC OCEAN

BRAZIL

PERU

CHILE

ARGENTINA

ATLANTIC OCEAN

2000 Miles
2000 Kilometers
1000
1000
0
0

N E S W

Mapping The World
The Spread of Imperialism, 1850–1914

The world's peoples interacted more in the late nineteenth century because of the spread of empire and increases in migration and travel. Behind this movement of peoples was the quest for opportunity and freedom, as well as ambition and greed. Occasionally those driving imperialism had philanthropic and scientific motives, but imperialists often used naked violence to achieve their ends.

Timeline

- **c. 1840–1900** Global migration because of indenture, imperial opportunity, and harsh environmental conditions
- **1857** Indian Uprising against the British
- **c. 1860–1900** Impressionism flourishes in the European arts, borrowing many non-Western techniques
- **1869** Suez Canal completed
- **c. 1870–1914** European powers, Japan, and the United States extend formal and informal control over Asia, Africa, and parts of Latin America
- **1876** British Parliament declares Victoria empress of India
- **1882** Britain takes over Egypt
- **1884–1885** European nations carve up Africa at the Berlin Conference
- **1894–1895** Sino-Japanese War
- **1898** Spanish–American War
- **1899–1900** Boxer Rebellion in China
- **1899–1902** South African War
- **1900** Sigmund Freud, *The Interpretation of Dreams*
- **1904–1905** Russo-Japanese War
- **1908** Young Turks' uprising against the Ottoman Empire
- **1910** Japan annexes Korea

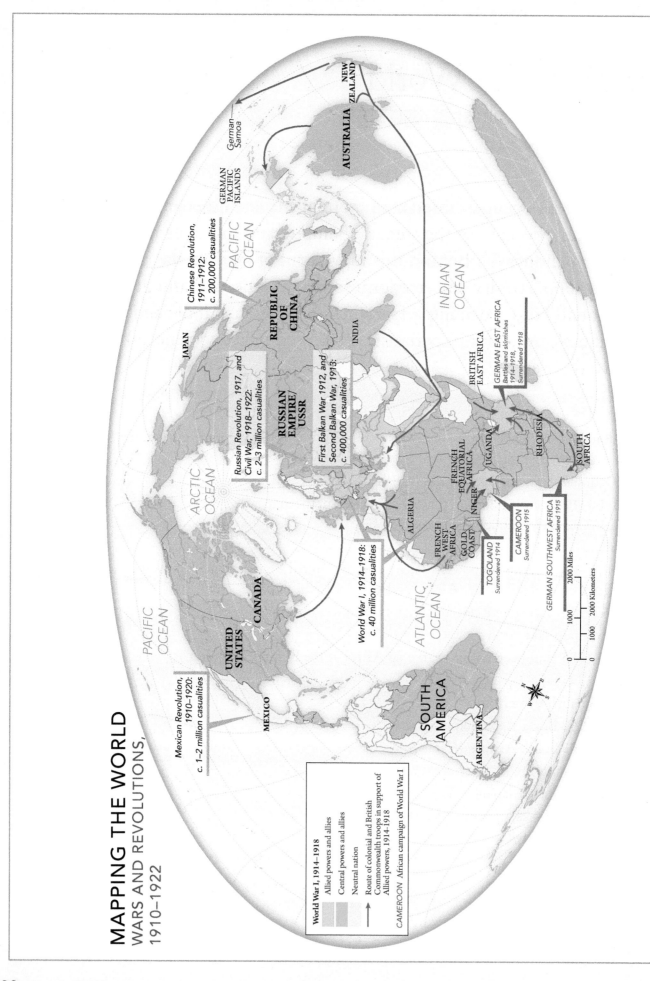

MAPPING THE WORLD
WARS AND REVOLUTIONS, 1910–1922

World War I, 1914–1918

- Allied powers and allies
- Central powers and allies
- Neutral nation
- → Route of colonial and British Commonwealth troops in support of Allied powers, 1914-1918

CAMEROON African campaign of World War I

Mexican Revolution, 1910–1920: c. 1–2 million casualties

Chinese Revolution, 1911–1912: c. 200,000 casualties

Russian Revolution, 1917, and Civil War, 1918-1922: c. 2–3 million casualties

First Balkan War 1912, and Second Balkan War, 1913: c. 400,000 casualties

World War I, 1914–1918: c. 40 million casualties

UNITED STATES

CANADA

MEXICO

SOUTH AMERICA

ARGENTINA

JAPAN

REPUBLIC OF CHINA

RUSSIAN EMPIRE/ USSR

INDIA

AUSTRALIA

NEW ZEALAND

German Samoa

GERMAN PACIFIC ISLANDS

ALGERIA

FRENCH WEST AFRICA

GOLD COAST

TOGOLAND *Surrendered 1914*

NIGER

CAMEROON *Surrendered 1915*

FRENCH EQUATORIAL AFRICA

UGANDA

BRITISH EAST AFRICA

GERMAN EAST AFRICA *Battles and skirmishes 1914-1918, Surrendered 1918*

RHODESIA

SOUTH AFRICA

GERMAN SOUTHWEST AFRICA *Surrendered 1915*

PACIFIC OCEAN

ARCTIC OCEAN

PACIFIC OCEAN

ATLANTIC OCEAN

INDIAN OCEAN

0   1000   2000 Miles
0   1000   2000 Kilometers

Mapping The World
Wars and Revolutions, 1910–1922

Wars and revolutions circled the globe in the early twentieth century. Areas where empire and imperial influence were at stake were especially hard hit, including a broad sweep of Eurasia. This era of local and global conflict brought dramatic political and other change, notably the fall of imperial dynasties, the exchange of colonial holdings and territory, and a stark toll in deaths from military campaigns, famine, and an influenza pandemic.

Timeline

- **1910** Mexican Revolution begins
- **1911–1912** Revolutionaries overthrow Qing dynasty in China
- **1912** First Balkan War
- **1913** Second Balkan War
- **1914** World War I begins
- **1917** Russian Revolution begins; United States enters World War I; Lenin returns to Russia
- **1918** Bolsheviks take full control of Russian government; Treaty of Brest-Litovsk; armistice ends World War I
- **1919** Germany forms Weimar Republic; May Fourth Movement in China
- **1919–1920** Treaties comprising Peace of Paris signed, including the Treaty of Versailles with Germany
- **1921** Lenin introduces New Economic Policy in Russia
- **1920s** Mohandas Gandhi's nonviolent movement for Indian independence attracts millions; mass culture flourishes in film and publishing industries; growth of radio transmissions; technology increases global productivity
- **1922** Civil war ends in Russia; Mussolini comes to power in Italy
- **1923** Founding of the independent republic of Turkey under Mustafa Kemal; formation of Union of Soviet Socialist Republics (USSR)

MAPPING THE WORLD
WORLD WAR II, 1937–1945

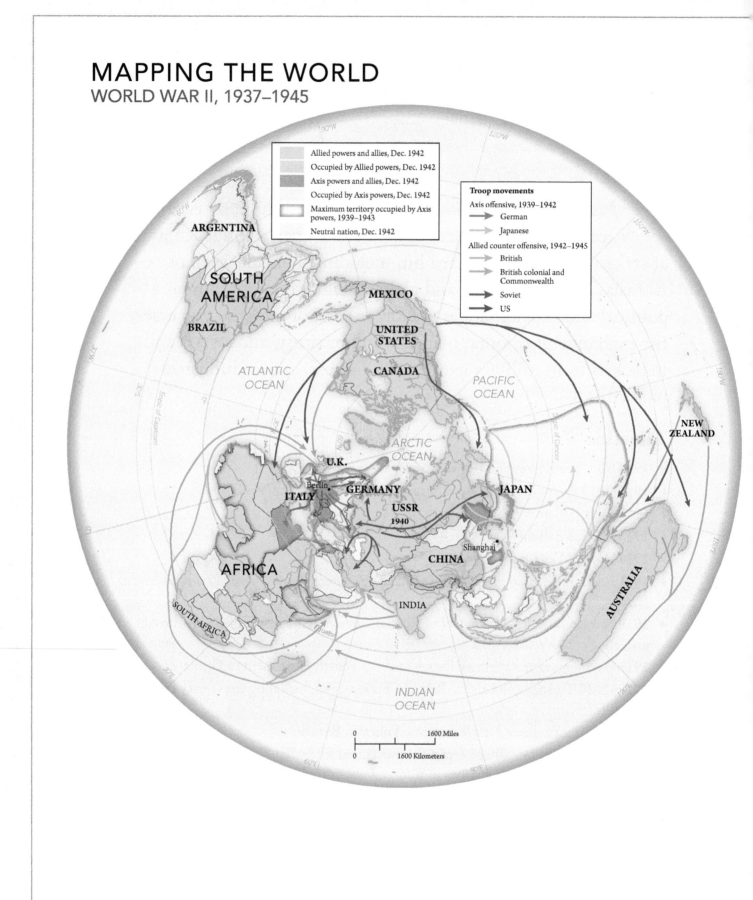

Allied powers and allies, Dec. 1942
Occupied by Allied powers, Dec. 1942
Axis powers and allies, Dec. 1942
Occupied by Axis powers, Dec. 1942
Maximum territory occupied by Axis powers, 1939–1943
Neutral nation, Dec. 1942

Troop movements
Axis offensive, 1939–1942
    German
    Japanese
Allied counter offensive, 1942–1945
    British
    British colonial and Commonwealth
    Soviet
    US

ARGENTINA

SOUTH AMERICA

BRAZIL

MEXICO

UNITED STATES

CANADA

ATLANTIC OCEAN

PACIFIC OCEAN

ARCTIC OCEAN

NEW ZEALAND

U.K.

Berlin

GERMANY

ITALY

USSR
1940

JAPAN

AFRICA

CHINA

Shanghai

SOUTH AFRICA

INDIA

AUSTRALIA

INDIAN OCEAN

Tropic of Cancer

Tropic of Capricorn

Equator

Arctic Circle

0   1600 Miles
0   1600 Kilometers

Mapping The World
World War II, 1937–1945

The Great Depression spread economic hardship, which was compounded by the advance of militarism and empire. Japan's drive to expand its empire early in the 1930s was followed by Italy's campaigns for empire in Africa and the German takeover of central and eastern Europe. These aspiring powers used increasingly formidable weaponry, lightning speed, and massive attacks on civilians. The culmination was World War II, which broke out in 1937 in East Asia and 1939 in Europe, ending only in 1945. The Great Depression and World War II stand out in human history as an era of unprecedented suffering.

Timeline

- **1920s** Collapse of commodity prices around the world
- **1929** Crash of the US stock market; global depression begins; Stalin's "liquidation of the kulaks"
- **1930** Gandhi's Salt March
- **1930s** Sweden begins setting up welfare state
- **1931** Japan invades Manchuria
- **1933** Hitler comes to power in Germany and ends representative government
- **1934** Chinese Communists begin Long March
- **1935** Nuremberg Laws against the Jews in Germany; Italy invades Ethiopia
- **1936** Purges and show trials begin in USSR
- **1937** Japan attacks China; World War II begins in Asia
- **1939** Germany invades Poland; World War II begins in Europe
- **1941** Germany invades USSR; Japan attacks Pearl Harbor; United States enters the war
- **1941–1945** Holocaust
- **1943** USSR defeats Germany at Stalingrad
- **1945** Fall of Berlin and surrender of Germany; United Nations charter signed; United States drops atomic bombs; Japan surrenders

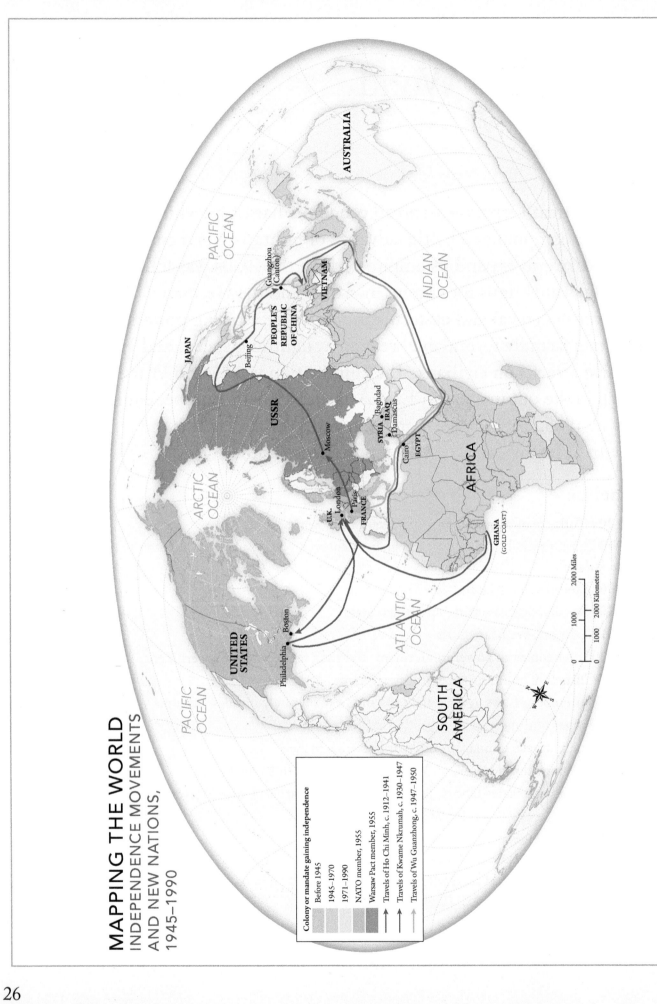

MAPPING THE WORLD
INDEPENDENCE MOVEMENTS AND NEW NATIONS, 1945–1990

Colony or mandate gaining independence

Before 1945
1945–1970
1971–1990

NATO member, 1955

Warsaw Pact member, 1955

Travels of Ho Chi Minh, c. 1912–1941

Travels of Kwame Nkrumah, c. 1930–1947

Travels of Wu Guanzhong, c. 1947–1950

PACIFIC OCEAN

AUSTRALIA

INDIAN OCEAN

Guangzhou (Canton)

VIETNAM

JAPAN

PEOPLE'S REPUBLIC OF CHINA

Beijing

USSR

Moscow

Baghdad

SYRIA   IRAQ   Damascus

Cairo   EGYPT

AFRICA

ARCTIC OCEAN

U.K.   London   Paris

FRANCE

GHANA (GOLD COAST)

UNITED STATES

Boston

Philadelphia

PACIFIC OCEAN

ATLANTIC OCEAN

SOUTH AMERICA

2000 Miles
2000 Kilometers
1000
1000
0
0

Mapping The World
Independence Movements and New Nations, 1945–1990

Earlier movements for freedom from colonialism were reinvigorated at the end of World War II; the Axis and Allied powers had been exhausted by this unprecedented conflict, and some were bankrupt. Independent nations emerged from the remnants of imperialism, some of them only after violent struggles with their rulers. These independent nations, however, faced a novel global situation—a bipolar world dominated by the Soviet Union and the United States and faced with a possible nuclear holocaust. This potentially disastrous confrontation was called the Cold War.

Timeline

- **1945** World War II ends
- **1947** India and Pakistan win independence
- **1948–1949** Arab–Israeli War
- **1948** Israel gains independence
- **1949** Communists take control of China; Western powers form the North Atlantic Treaty Organization; USSR detonates atomic bomb
- **1949** Indonesia gains independence
- **1950–1953** Korean War
- **1952** Egypt achieves full independence under Nasser
- **1953** Death of Stalin
- **1954** Vietnamese defeat French army at Dien Bien Phu
- **1956** Khrushchev denounce Stalin; Suez crisis; revolution in Hungary
- **1957** USSR launches *Sputnik*
- **1958** Khrushchev forces Boris Pasternak to refuse Nobel Prize in Literature
- **1961** Construction of the Berlin Wall
- **1962** Algeria wins independence; Cuban Missile Crisis
- **c. 1966–1976** Mao Zedong's "Cultural Revolution"

MAPPING THE WORLD
OPEC, PACIFIC TIGERS, AND GLOBAL MIGRATIONS, 1960–1990

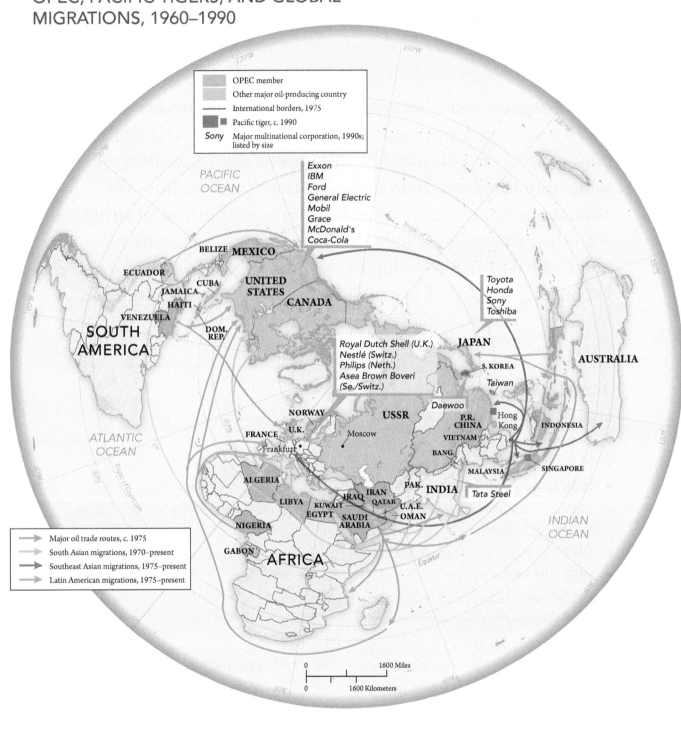

Legend:
- OPEC member
- Other major oil-producing country
- International borders, 1975
- Pacific tiger, c. 1990
- *Sony* Major multinational corporation, 1990s; listed by size

Exxon
IBM
Ford
General Electric
Mobil
Grace
McDonald's
Coca-Cola

Toyota
Honda
Sony
Toshiba

Royal Dutch Shell (U.K.)
Nestlé (Switz.)
Philips (Neth.)
Asea Brown Boveri (Se./Switz.)

Daewoo

Tata Steel

PACIFIC OCEAN

ATLANTIC OCEAN

INDIAN OCEAN

BELIZE
MEXICO
ECUADOR
CUBA
JAMAICA
HAITI
VENEZUELA
DOM. REP.
SOUTH AMERICA
UNITED STATES
CANADA

NORWAY
FRANCE
U.K.
Frankfurt
Moscow
USSR
P.R. CHINA
VIETNAM
BANG.
JAPAN
S. KOREA
Taiwan
Hong Kong
AUSTRALIA
INDONESIA
SINGAPORE
MALAYSIA
INDIA
PAK.
IRAN
IRAQ
QATAR
U.A.E.
OMAN
KUWAIT
EGYPT
SAUDI ARABIA
LIBYA
ALGERIA
NIGERIA
GABON
AFRICA

Tropic of Cancer
Equator
Tropic of Capricorn

- Major oil trade routes, c. 1975
- South Asian migrations, 1970–present
- Southeast Asian migrations, 1975–present
- Latin American migrations, 1975–present

0   1600 Miles
0   1600 Kilometers

28

Mapping The World
OPEC, Pacific Tigers, and Global Migrations, 1960–1990

In the decades from 1960 to 1990, the world seemed bogged down in the Cold War order, but it was actually in tremendous flux. Technological change was transforming society and would continue to do so through the twenty-first century. Economic power was beginning to shift away from the West, and this shift would accelerate over the coming decades. Finally, under the influence of technology and global economic change, livelihoods became postindustrial in some areas and more attuned to manufacturing in formerly agricultural regions.

Timeline

- **1957** USSR launches *Sputnik*
- **1963** Betty Friedan, *The Feminine Mystique*
- **1967** Arab–Israeli Six-Day War
- **1968** "Prague Spring" in Czechoslovakia
- **1969** US astronauts land on moon
- **1972** US president Richard Nixon visits China; SALT I agreement
- **1973** Arab–Israeli Yom Kippur War; OPEC raises oil prices and imposes embargo
- **1973–1976** Aleksandr Solzhenitsyn, *Gulag Archipelago*
- **1975** Vietnam War ends; Vietnam reunited
- **1978** World's first test-tube baby born
- **1978–1979** Islamic revolution in Iran
- **1979–1989** Soviet war in Afghanistan
- **1980** Solidarity labor union organizes resistance to communism in Poland; prime minister Margaret Thatcher introduces neoliberal program in Britain
- **1985** Mikhail Gorbachev becomes Soviet leader, introduces new policies of perestroika and glasnost
- **1989** Chinese students demonstrate at Tiananmen Square; communist regimes in eastern Europe fall
- **1992** Soviet Union no longer exists

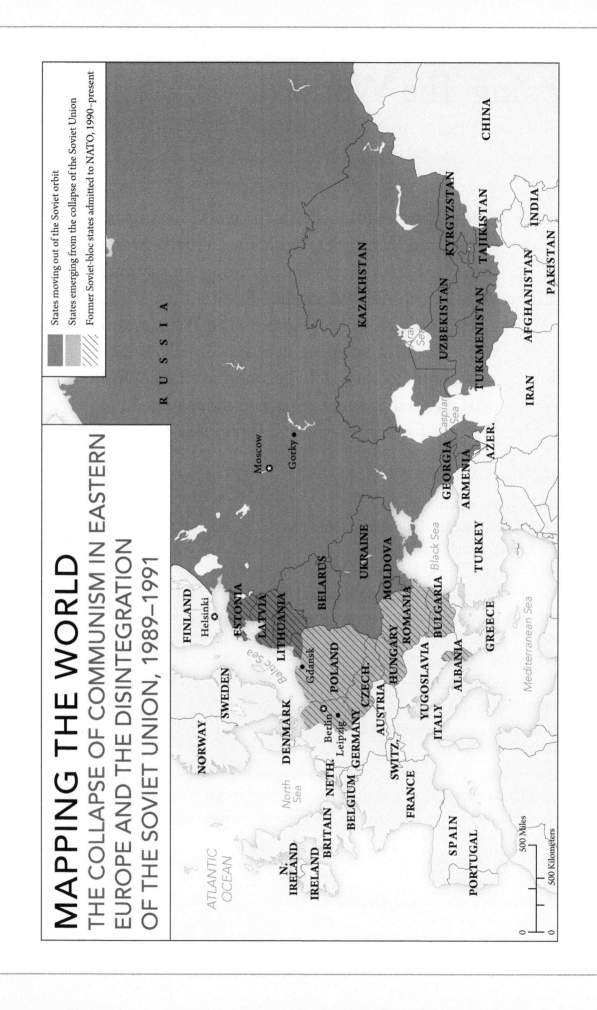

MAPPING THE WORLD
THE COLLAPSE OF COMMUNISM IN EASTERN EUROPE AND THE DISINTEGRATION OF THE SOVIET UNION, 1989–1991

States moving out of the Soviet orbit

States emerging from the collapse of the Soviet Union

Former Soviet-bloc states admitted to NATO, 1990–present

RUSSIA

CHINA

KYRGYZSTAN

TAJIKISTAN

INDIA

PAKISTAN

KAZAKHSTAN

UZBEKISTAN

TURKMENISTAN

AFGHANISTAN

IRAN

Aral Sea

Caspian Sea

AZER.

GEORGIA

ARMENIA

Moscow

Gorky

TURKEY

GREECE

Black Sea

BULGARIA

ROMANIA

MOLDOVA

UKRAINE

BELARUS

ALBANIA

YUGOSLAVIA

ITALY

HUNGARY

AUSTRIA

CZECH

POLAND

Gdansk

LITHUANIA

LATVIA

ESTONIA

FINLAND

Helsinki

Baltic Sea

Mediterranean Sea

SWITZ.

FRANCE

GERMANY

Berlin

Leipzig

BELGIUM

NETH.

DENMARK

SWEDEN

NORWAY

BRITAIN

IRELAND

N. IRELAND

North Sea

ATLANTIC OCEAN

SPAIN

PORTUGAL

500 Miles

500 Kilometers

0

0

Mapping The World
The Collapse of Communism in Eastern Europe and the
Disintegration of the Soviet Union, 1989–1991

The sudden collapse of the Soviet Empire in 1989 and the subsequent end of the USSR itself in December 1991 brought an end to the Cold War. More important to those in the region, it meant social, economic, and political change. The new Russian nation, however, remained influential as it began drawing on and marketing its natural resources more effectively. Russia's "near abroad"—the lands once part of the USSR or within the post–World War II Soviet sphere of influence—is a complicated place where the Soviet legacy weighs heavily.

Timeline

- **March 1989** Parliamentary elections in the USSR spur autonomy and independence demands
- **November 1989** Berlin Wall falls
- **June 1989** Solidarity wins elections in Poland
- **October–November 1989** Protests overwhelm Communists in Czechoslovakia
- **December 1989** Romania: Nicolae Ceauşescu overthrown and executed
- **March–April 1990** Free elections sweep Communists from power in Hungary
- **June 1990** Reformers win in free elections in Bulgaria
- **October 1990** East and West Germany reunified
- **December 1991** Soviet Union dissolves

MAPPING THE WORLD
LINES OF CONFLICT IN THE MUSLIM WORLD

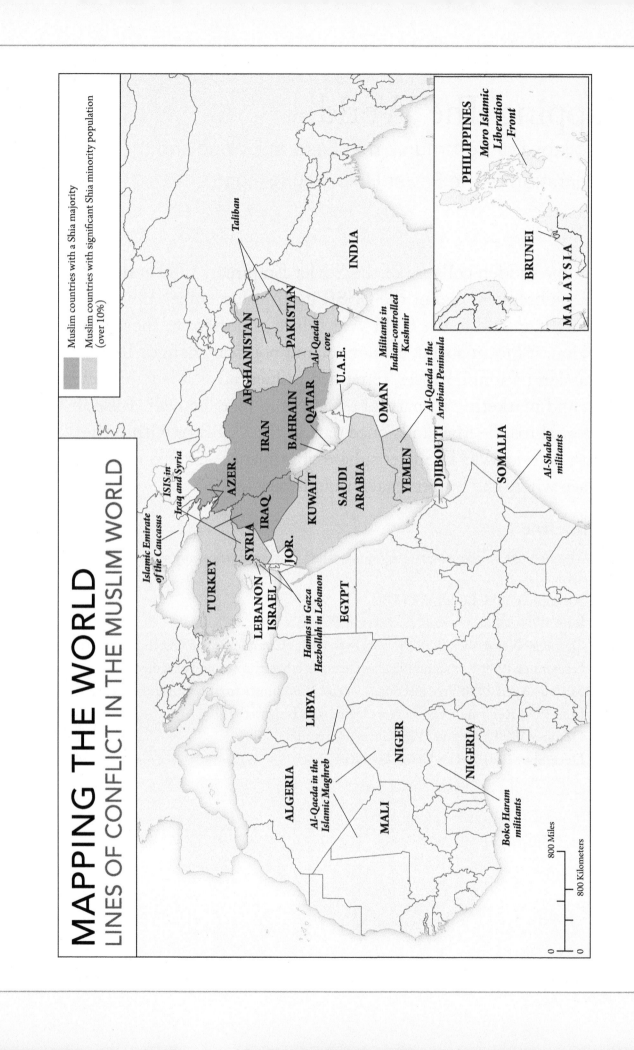

Muslim countries with a Shia majority

Muslim countries with significant Shia minority population (over 10%)

PHILIPPINES
Moro Islamic Liberation Front

BRUNEI

MALAYSIA

Taliban

INDIA

AFGHANISTAN

PAKISTAN

Al-Qaeda core

U.A.E.

IRAN

BAHRAIN

QATAR

Militants in Indian-controlled Kashmir

AZER.

OMAN

Islamic Emirate of the Caucasus

ISIS in Iraq and Syria

IRAQ

KUWAIT

SAUDI ARABIA

YEMEN

DJIBOUTI

Al-Qaeda in the Arabian Peninsula

SOMALIA

Al-Shabab militants

TURKEY

SYRIA

LEBANON

ISRAEL

JOR.

EGYPT

Hamas in Gaza Hezbollah in Lebanon

LIBYA

ALGERIA

Al-Qaeda in the Islamic Maghreb

MALI

NIGER

NIGERIA

Boko Haram militants

800 Miles

800 Kilometers

0

0

Mapping The World
Lines of Conflict in the Muslim World

Two deeply contentious fault lines have emerged within predominantly Muslim countries. One is the friction between Sunni and Shia populations. Shia majorities have run roughshod over Sunni minorities in Iran and Iraq. In Bahrain, Saudi Arabia, Yemen, and Pakistan, the situation is reversed, with Shia minorities suffering discrimination and violence at the hands of Sunnis. Sunni insurgents have opened the second fault line with militant challenges to the political status quo, from Nigeria to Syria and Iraq, to Afghanistan and even the Philippines.

Timeline

- **1979** Islamist-led revolution topples Shah in Iran
- **1980–1988** Iran–Iraq War
- **1985** Hezbollah organized in southern Lebanon
- **1987** First *intifada* against Israel
- **1988** Hamas founded in Gaza
- **1989** National Islamic Front seizes power in Sudan
- **1990** Saddam Hussein invades Kuwait, but driven out by US-led coalition
- **1996** Taliban takes control in Kabul, Afghanistan
- **1998** Osama bin Laden declares all Americans a target of *jihad*
- **2000** Hezbollah drives Israel out of southern Lebanon; second *intifada* against Israel
- **2001** Al-Qaeda attack against United States; Taliban overthrown in Afghanistan
- **2003** United States deposes Saddam Hussein in Iraq
- **2007** Hamas seizes full control of Gaza
- **2008** Israel invades Gaza
- **2011** Arab Spring; civil war erupts in Syria and Yemen; bin Laden killed by US forces
- **2013** Army coup in Egypt deposes Muhammad Morsi
- **2014** ISIS controls large swathes of Syrian and Iraq
- **2018** United States cancels nuclear deal with Iran; American embassy moved to Jerusalem

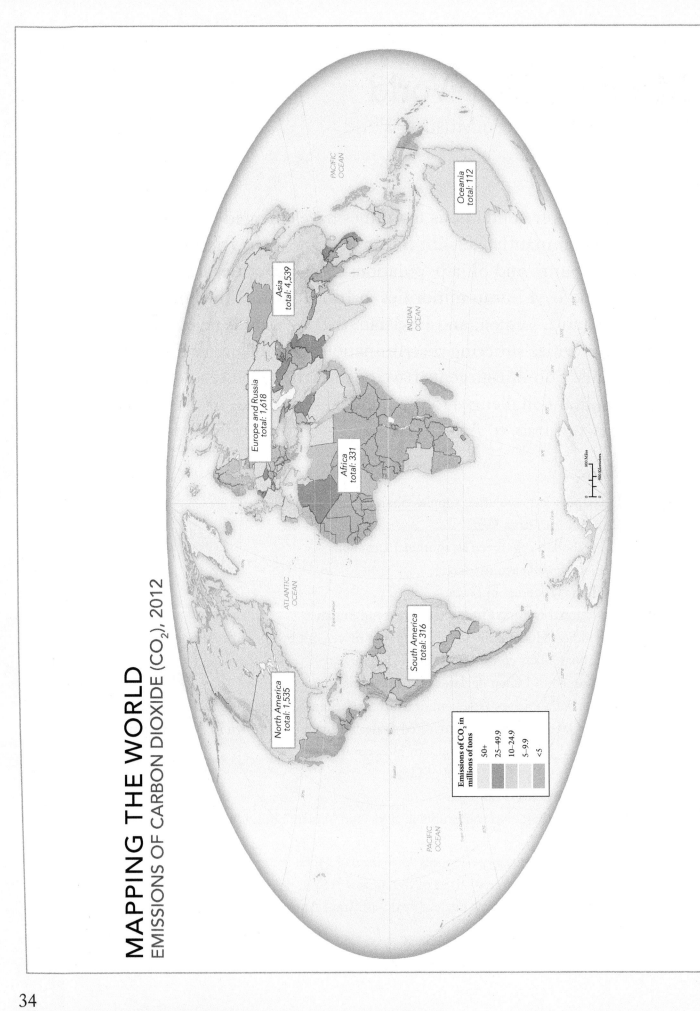

MAPPING THE WORLD
EMISSIONS OF CARBON DIOXIDE (CO₂), 2012

Asia
total: 4,539

Europe and Russia
total: 1,618

Africa
total: 331

Oceania
total: 112

North America
total: 1,535

South America
total: 316

PACIFIC
OCEAN

INDIAN
OCEAN

ATLANTIC
OCEAN

PACIFIC
OCEAN

**Emissions of CO₂ in
millions of tons**

50+
25–49.9
10–24.9
5–9.9
<5

900 Miles

900 Kilometers

Mapping The World

Emissions of Carbon Dioxide (CO_2), 2012

Carbon dioxide has been the major driver for both global warming and ocean acidification. It has entered the atmosphere in ever-greater amounts, primarily as a result of human activity, either through burning fossil fuels or by destroying forests. Some countries have much higher total output than others. There are also striking regional differences. East Asia's total emissions of carbon dioxide is more than twice that of Europe and Russia, nearly 3 times that of North America, and 13 times that of Africa.

Item	Increase factor
Total world population	4
World urban population	13
World economy	14
Industrial output	40
Coal production	7
Carbon dioxide emissions	17
Water use	9
Marine fish catch	35
Cattle population	4
Pig population	9

Environmental Change, 1890s–1990s

Source: Adapted from J. R. McNeil, *Something New under the Sun: An Environmental History of the Twentieth Century World* (New York: W. W. Norton, 2000), 360.

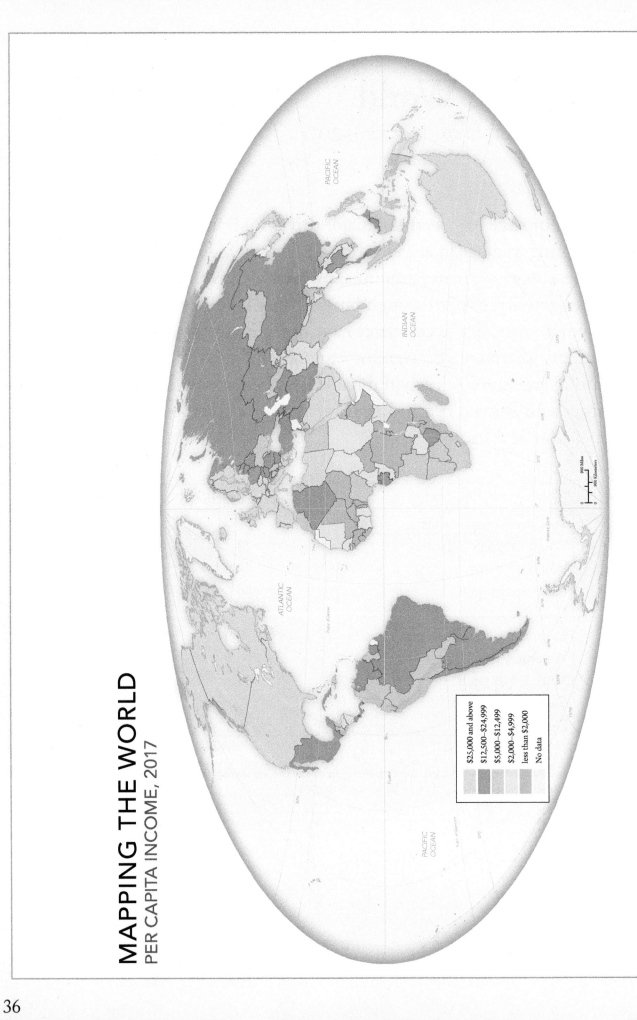

MAPPING THE WORLD
PER CAPITA INCOME, 2017

PACIFIC OCEAN

INDIAN OCEAN

ATLANTIC OCEAN

PACIFIC OCEAN

$25,000 and above
$12,500–$24,999
$5,000–$12,499
$2,000–$4,999
less than $2,000
No data

900 Miles
900 Kilometers

Mapping The World
Per Capita Income, 2017

Income and wealth generated by globalization have not been distributed equally among the world's countries. Despite impressive economic growth in the past few decades, India and China have failed to catch up with the United States, western Europe, and Japan. In Latin America, Brazil and Mexico have increased the per capita incomes of their populaces, while most of sub-Saharan Africa remains poor. The wealth of many Middle Eastern countries is dependent on oil, a resource that likely will become scarce in the future.

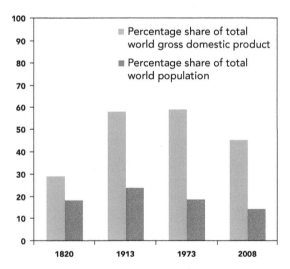

Concentration of wealth in the developed world, 1820–2008.
(The developed world is defined as western Europe, the United States, Canada, Australia, New Zealand, and Japan.) *Source:* Data from Angus Maddison, "Historical Statistics of the World Economy: 1-2008 AD" https://www.rug.nl/ggdc/historicaldevelopment/maddison/

Outline Maps

Starting Points: Find Your Place in the World

✳ ✳ ✳

1. Find and color in these places:
   a. The state or country where you were born
   b. The state where you are now living

2. Identify and label the following places:
   a. The capital of the state where you are now living
   b. Canada
   c. Mexico
   d. Africa
   e. Europe
   f. Asia
   g. Australia
   h. South America
   i. Atlantic Ocean
   j. Pacific Ocean
   k. Indian Ocean
   l. Mediterranean Sea

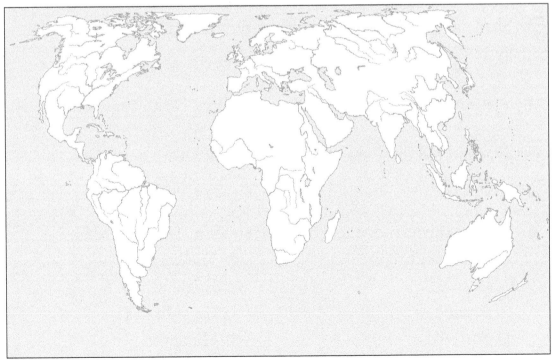

Starting Points: Find Your Place in the World

Name: _____ Date: _____

Europe and the Greater Mediterranean, 1346–1453

✳ ✳ ✳

1. Label:
   a. Sarai
   b. Caffa
   c. Constantinople (Istanbul)
   d. Genoa
   e. Venice
   f. Florence
   g. Paris
   h. London
   i. Barcelona
   j. Lisbon
   k. Cracow
   l. Danzig
   m. Moscow
   n. Bruges
   o. Nuremburg
   p. Rome
   q. Naples
   r. Cairo
   s. Tunis
   t. Damascus

2. Shade in tan those areas where the Black Death appeared in 1346.

3. Shade in yellow those areas where the Black Death appeared by 1348.

4. Shade in orange those areas where the Black Death appeared by 1350.

5. Shade in red those areas where the Black Death appeared after 1350.

6. Outline the territory held by these states in 1453 and label:
   a. Ottoman Empire
   b. Castile
   c. Aragon
   d. Portugal
   e. Granada
   f. Holy Roman Empire
   g. France
   h. England
   i. Papal States
   j. Hungary
   k. Naples
   l. Poland-Lithuania

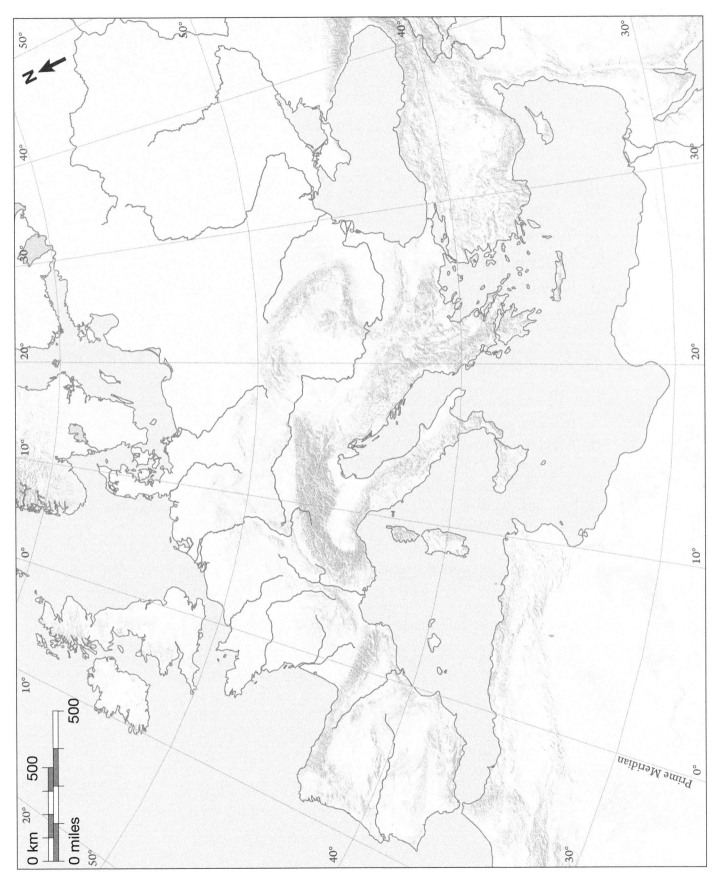

Europe and the Greater Mediterranean, 1346–1453

Name: _____ Date: _____

The Aztec Empire, 1325–1521

✳ ✳ ✳

1. Label these places and geographical features with a black pencil:

   a. Tabasco
   b. Yucatan Peninsula
   c. Valley of Mexico
   d. Sierra Madre Oriental
   e. Sierra Madre del Sur
   f. Maya Highlands
   g. Gulf of Mexico
   h. Pacific Ocean
   i. Caribbean Sea
   j. Tenochtitlán

2. Identify the location of these peoples and label with a red pencil:

   a. Mexica (Aztec)
   b. Mixtec
   c. Tlaxcalan
   d. Tarascan
   e. Zapotec
   f. Maya

3. Use a yellow pencil to shade in Aztec territory by 1440.

4. Use an orange pencil to shade in Aztec territory by 1481.

5. Use a green pencil to shade in Aztec territory by 1521.

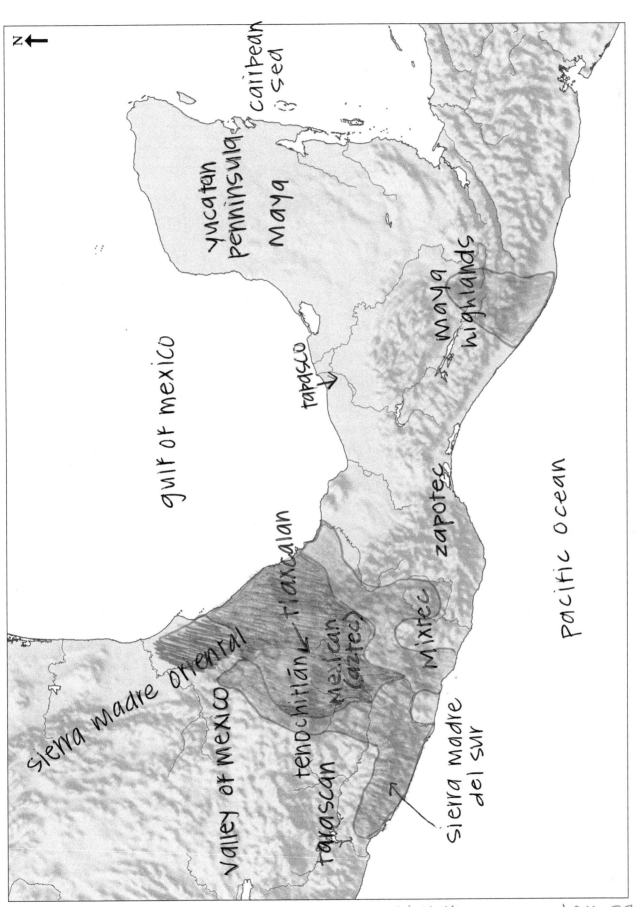

The Aztec Empire, 1325–1521

Copyright © 2019 Oxford University Press

Name: Natalie Hell

Date: Jan. 27

The Inca Empire, 1325–1521

✳ ✳ ✳

1. Locate and label these places and geographical features with a black pencil:
   a. Andes Mountains
   b. Pacific Ocean
   c. Cuzco
   d. Lake Titicaca
   e. Machu Picchu
   f. Chan Chan
   g. Quito
   h. Tiwanaku
   i. Amazon River

2. Draw a dotted line to indicate the Tropic of Capricorn and a solid line to indicate the equator.

3. Locate and label these peoples with a blue pencil:
   a. Chanka
   b. Chimú
   c. Canaris
   d. Mapuche
   e. Chachapoyas

4. With a red pencil, show Inca territory by 1440.

5. With an orange pencil, show Inca territory by 1471.

6. With a yellow pencil, show Inca territory by 1493.

7. With a green pencil, show Inca territory by 1525.

8. Draw lines to indicate the Inca road network.

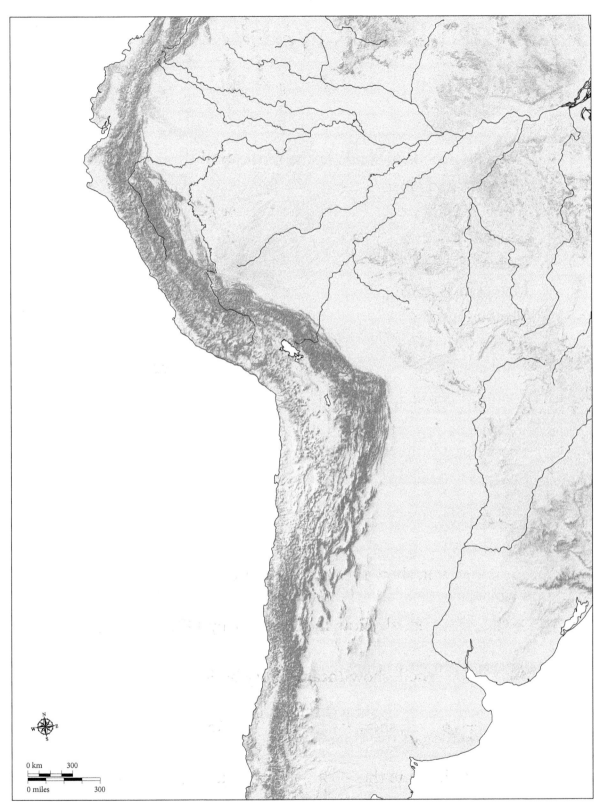

0 km   300

0 miles   300

The Inca Empire, 1325–1521

Name: _____   Date: _____

Voyages of Discovery, 1405–1600

✳ ✳ ✳

1. Use colored pencils to shade in the territory of these states and empires and label:
   a. Ming Empire
   b. Mughal Empire
   c. Safavid Empire
   d. Ottoman Empire
   e. Russian Empire
   f. France
   g. England
   h. Spanish Empire, including claims in the New World, c. 1600
   i. Portuguese Empire, including claims in Africa, India, Southeast Asia, and the New World, c. 1600

2. Draw red arrows to show the voyages of Zheng He between 1405 and 1433.

3. Draw blue arrows to show Columbus's first transatlantic voyage in 1492–1493.

4. Draw green arrows to show da Gama's voyage in 1497–1498.

5. Draw brown arrows to show Magellan's and del Cano's circumnavigation of the globe in 1519–1522.

6. Draw the line demarcated by the Treaty of Tordesillas in 1494.

7. Label:
   Madeira Islands, Canary Islands, Azores, Cape Verde Islands, Benin, Congo, Angola, Brazil, Mexico, Peru, Cuba, Cape of Good Hope, Calicut, Cuzco, Tenochtitlán, Melaka, East Indies, West Indies, Aden, Hormuz, Muscat

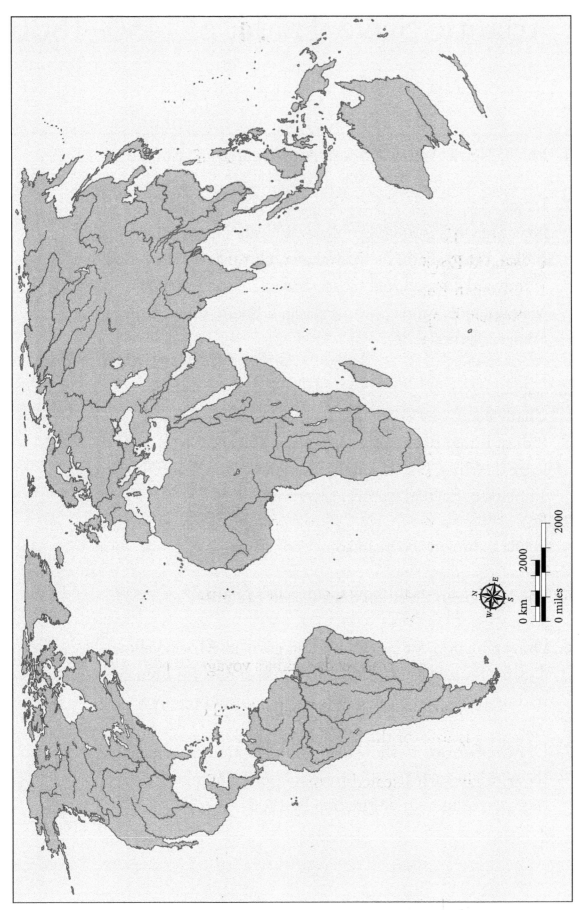

Voyages of Discovery, 1405–1600   Name: _____   Date: _____

The Atlantic Slave Trade, c. 1450–1800

* * *

1. Label: North America, South America, Africa, Europe

2. Label:
   New France, Virginia, Carolinas, Florida New Spain, West Indies, Brazil, Peru, New Granada, Guyana, Senegambia, Windward Coast, Gold Coast, Slave Coast, Angola, Mozambique, Madagascar, Portugal, Spain, Great Britain, France, Netherlands

3. Label:
   Charleston, New Orleans, Mexico City, Cartagena de Indies, Lima, Recife, Rio de Janeiro, Buenos Aires, São Jorge da Mina, Gao, Luanda, Benguela, Jenne-jeno, Lisbon, Timbuktu, Seville, Nantes, Liverpool

4. Shade in brown the main sources of slaves.

5. Shade in green the main destinations of slaves.

6. Draw pink dots for British trading ports in Africa, yellow dots for Portuguese trading ports, purple dots for French trading ports, and orange dots for Dutch trading ports.

7. Draw red arrows to show the main slave trade routes. Make the width of each arrow correspond to the number of slaves transported to each destination by 1800.

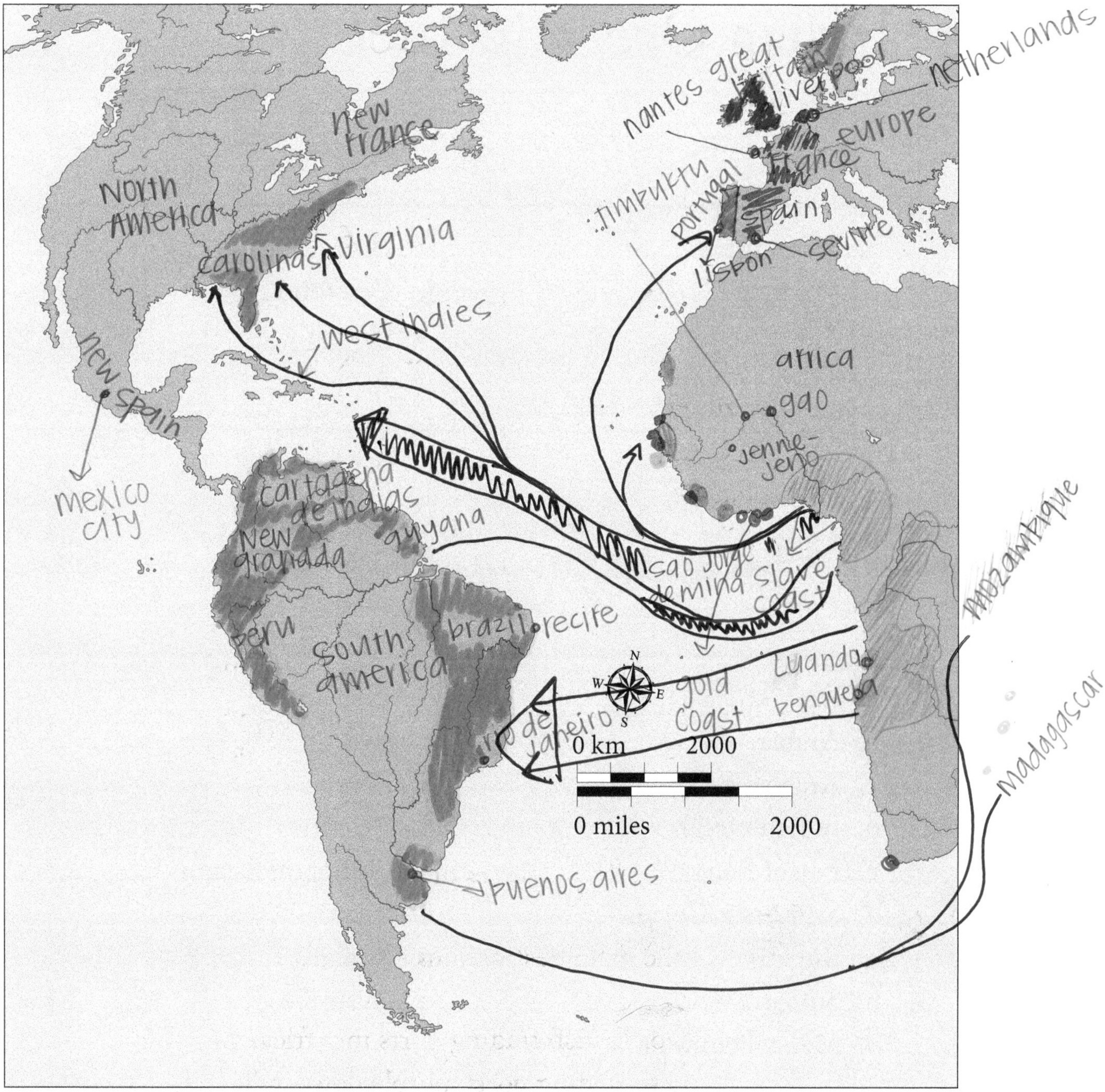
new france
North America
carolinas
virginia
west indies
new spain
mexico city
cartagena de indias
New granada
guyana
peru
south america
brazil
recife
rio de janeiro
buenos aires
N
W
E
S
0 km
2000
0 miles
2000
nantes
great britain
liverpool
netherlands
europe
france
portugal
spain
lisbon
seville
timbuktu
africa
gao
jenne-jeno
sao jorge de mina
slave coast
gold coast
Luanda
benguela
mozambique
madagascar

The Atlantic Slave Trade, c. 1450–1800

Name: natalie H. **Date:** ________

- main source
- main destinations
- british trading post
- portugese
- french
- dutch

The Indian Ocean in 1600

* * *

1. Label these trading ports:
   a. Mogadishu
   b. Malindi
   c. Zanzibar
   d. Kilwa
   e. Sofala
   f. Cambay
   g. Calicut
   h. Aden
   i. Goa

   j. Hormuz
   k. Colombo
   l. Hooghly
   m. Aceh
   n. Melaka
   o. Bantam
   p. Macao
   q. Nagasaki
   r. Manila

2. Label
   a. East Africa
   b. Arabia
   c. Arabian Sea
   d. Indian Ocean
   e. Bay of Bengal
   f. Sri Lanka/Ceylon
   g. Burma
   h. Sumatra
   i. Malay Peninsula

   j. Vietnam
   k. Java
   l. Borneo
   m. Celebes
   n. Philippine Islands
   o. Japan
   p. Korea
   q. Australia

3. Use different colored pencils to shade and label these empires:
   a. Safavid
   b. Ottoman (only partially visible)
   c. Mughal
   d. Ming

4. Shade in the territory controlled or claimed by Portugal in 1600.

5. Draw a solid black line to show Portuguese trading routes.

6. Draw dotted black lines to show the route of Spanish galleons from Mexico.

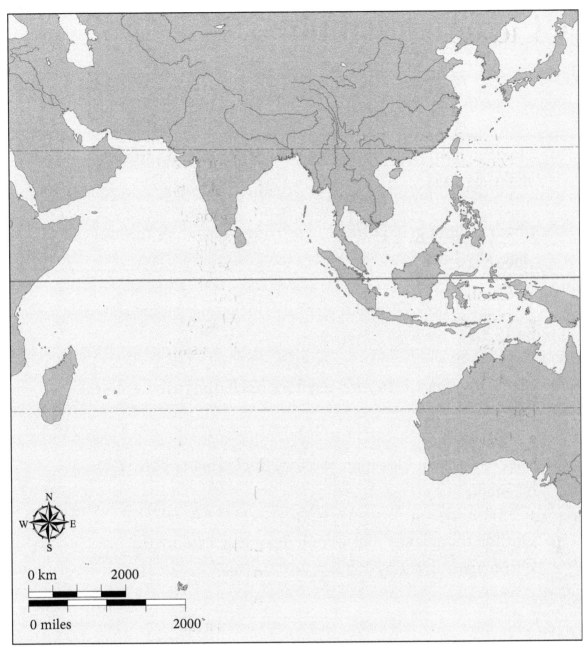

The Indian Ocean in 1600

Name: _____   Date: _____

The Ottoman Empire, 1453–1683

* * *

1. Shade in dark green Ottoman territory (including tribute states) by 1453.

2. Shade in light green Ottoman territory (including tribute states) by 1488.

3. Shade in yellow Ottoman territory (including tribute states) by 1520.

4. Shade in orange Ottoman territory (including tribute states) by 1566.

5. Shade in brown Ottoman territory (including tribute states) by 1683.

6. Outline those lands that were temporarily held by the Ottomans but lost by 1683.

7. Label:
   a. Istanbul
   b. Anatolia
   c. Bulgaria
   d. Greece
   e. Mesopotamia
   f. Egypt
   g. Tripoli
   h. Tunis
   i. Algiers
   j. Albania
   k. Balkan Mountains
   l. Georgia
   m. Caucasus Mountains
   n. Crimea
   o. Moldovia
   p. Transylvania
   q. Hungary
   r. Bosnia
   s. Budapest
   t. Vienna
   u. The Hijaz
   v. Mecca
   w. Yemen
   x. Baghdad

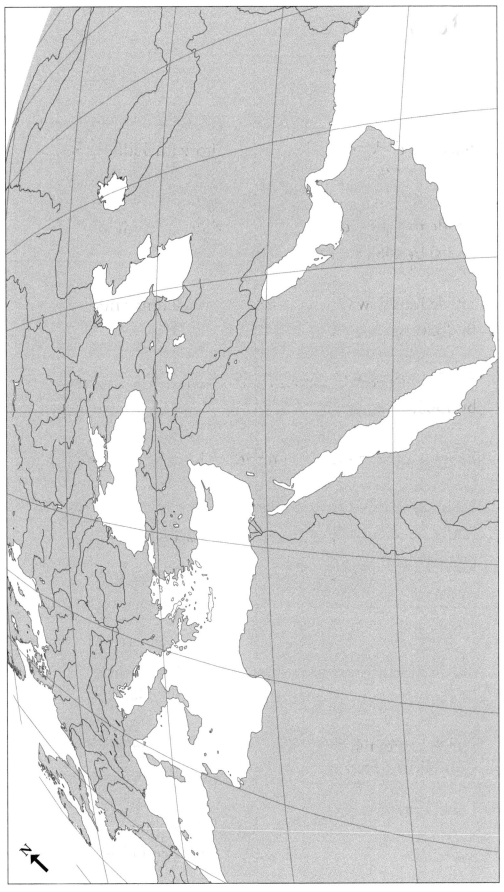

**The Ottoman Empire,
1453–1683**

Name: _____   Date: _____

The Reformation

* * *

1. Label the following European states and provinces, c. 1580:
   a. Portugal
   b. Spain
   c. Navarre
   d. France
   e. Alsace
   f. Savoy
   g. Austria
   h. Bavaria
   i. Saxony
   j. Brandenburg
   k. Mecklenburg
   l. Spanish Netherlands
   m. United Provinces
   n. Pomerania
   o. England
   p. Ireland
   q. Scotland
   r. Italy
   s. Ottoman Empire
   t. Hungary
   u. Bohemia
   v. Poland-Lithuania
   w. Russia
   x. Norway
   y. Sweden
   z. Holy Roman Empire

2. Keeping in mind that many areas had a mix of different faiths, shade in yellow those territories that were predominantly Lutheran in 1580.

3. Shade in orange those territories that were predominantly Anglican in 1580.

4. Shade in blue those areas that were predominantly Calvinist in 1580.

5. Shade in green those areas that were predominantly Roman Catholic in 1580.

6. Label these cities:
   a. Worms
   b. Trent
   c. Nantes
   d. Rome
   e. Paris
   f. Wittenberg
   g. Geneva
   h. Loyola

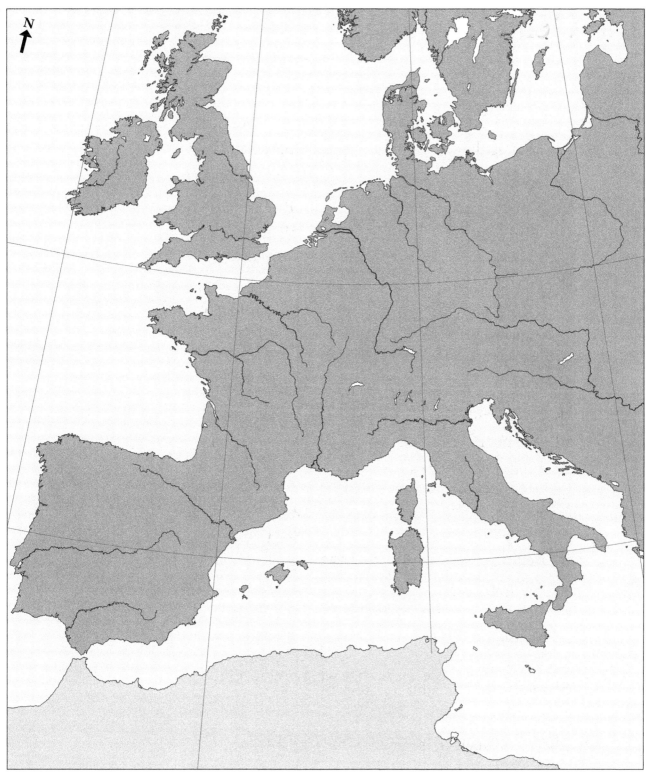

The Reformation

Name: _____ Date: _____

The Qing Dynasty, 1644–1799

✳ ✳ ✳

1. Label the following regions, rivers, and cities:

   Regions:

   a. Manchuria
   b. Mongolia
   c. Xingjiang
   d. Tibet
   e. Russia
   f. Japan
   g. Taiwan
   h. Burma
   i. Vietnam
   j. Siam (Thailand)
   k. Bhutan

   Rivers:

   a. Amur
   b. Yellow
   c. Yangzi

   Cities:

   a. Urumchi
   b. Beijing
   c. Kaifeng
   d. Xi'an
   e. Nanjing
   f. Hangzhou
   g. Fuzhou
   h. Guangzhou
   i. Macao
   j. Lhasa

2. Shade in red Manchu territory by 1644.

3. Shade in orange Manchu territory by 1659.

4. Shade in yellow Manchu territory by 1697.

5. Shade in brown Manchu territory by 1760.

6. Shade in blue tributary states.

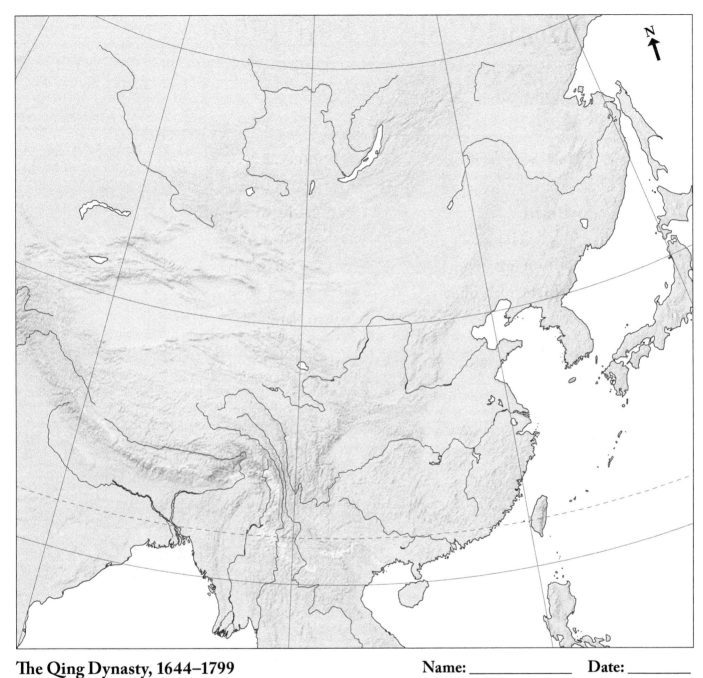

The Qing Dynasty, 1644–1799

Name: _____   Date: _____

New World Colonies in 1750

* * *

1. Label these territories:
   a. Peru
   b. Brazil
   c. New Mexico
   d. New Granada
   e. Thirteen colonies
   f. New France
   g. Saint-Domingue
   h. Cuba
   i. New Spain
   j. Guyana
   k. Suriname
   l. Louisiana
   m. Jamaica
   n. Florida

2. Label these cities/towns:
   a. Mexico City
   b. Rio de Janeiro
   c. Buenos Aires
   d. Lima
   e. Bogotá
   f. Cartagena de Indias
   g. Charleston
   h. New York
   i. Havana
   j. Potosí
   k. Acapulco
   l. Quebec
   m. Zacatecas
   n. St. Augustine

3. Shade British-controlled territories in pink.

4. Shade Dutch-controlled territories in orange.

5. Shade French-controlled territories in blue.

6. Shade Spanish-controlled territories in red.

7. Shade Portuguese-controlled territories in yellow.

New World Colonies in 1750

Copyright © 2019 Oxford University Press

Name: _____ Date: _____

Wars and Revolutions in the Atlantic World, 1750–1830

* * *

Map A

1. Label these European powers as they appeared in 1750:
   a. Great Britain
   b. France
   c. Portugal
   d. Spain
   e. Netherlands
   f. Austria
   g. Russia
   h. Ottoman Empire

2. Shade and label those European colonies that gained independence by 1830. Use red for former British colonics, blue for former French colonies, green for former Spanish colonies, and orange for former Portuguese colonies.

3. Mark with black dots and label those European colonies that did not gain independence by 1830.

Map B

1. Mark with an X these major battles of the Napoleonic Wars: Marengo, Trafalgar, Austerlitz, Jena, Friedland, Wagram, Borodino, Waterloo

2. Draw the boundaries of these European states after the Congress of Vienna:
   a. German confederation
   b. France
   c. Austrian Empire
   d. Russian Empire
   e. Piedmont-Sardinia
   f. Prussia
   g. Netherlands

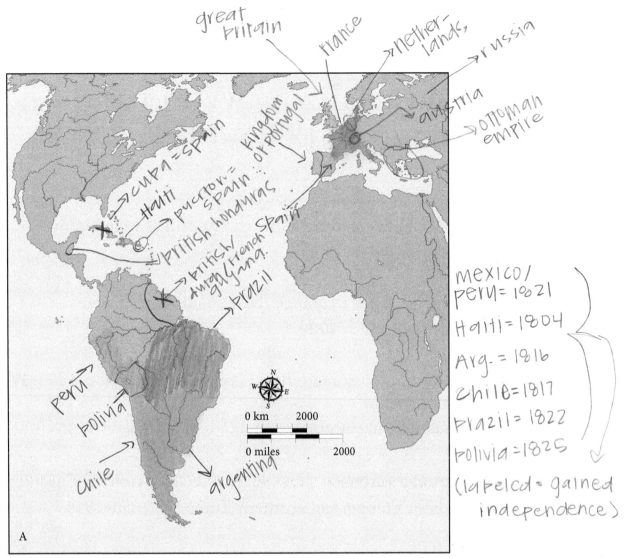

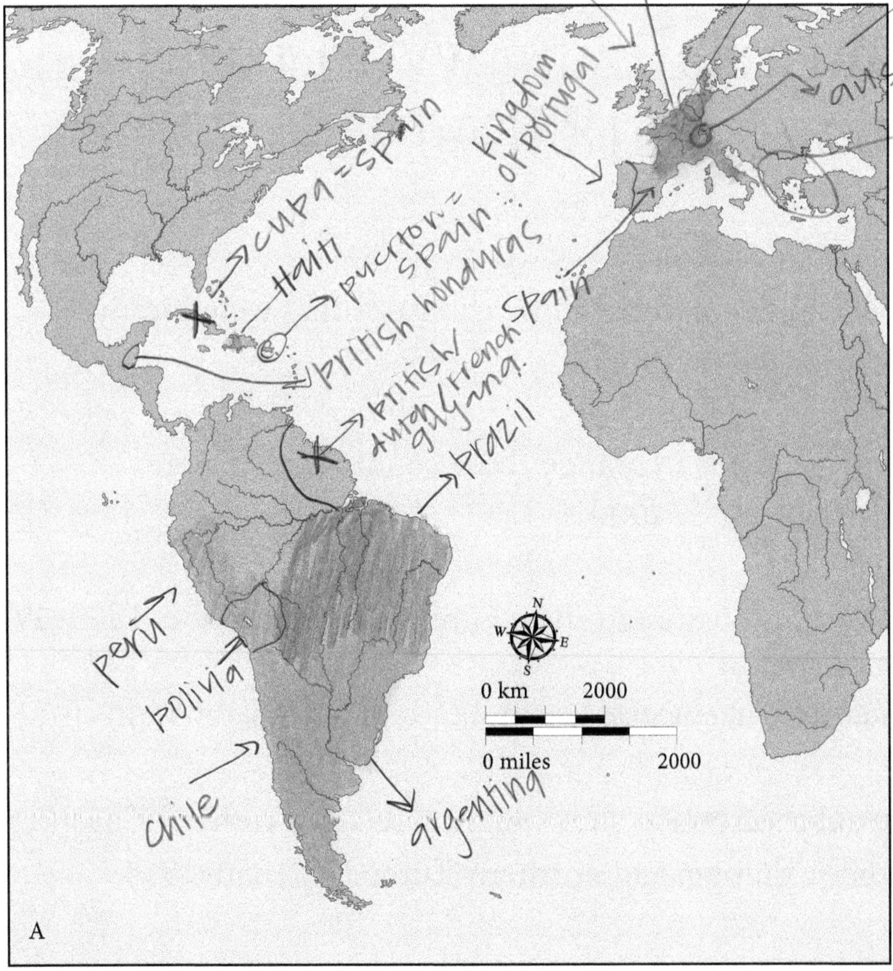
great britain
france
netherlands
russia
austria
ottoman empire
kingdom of portugal
cuba = spain
Haiti
puerto = spain
british honduras
Spain
british/dutch/french guyana
brazil
peru
bolivia
chile
argentina
N
W
E
S
0 km
2000
0 miles
2000
A
mexico/peru = 1821
Haiti = 1804
Arg. = 1816
chile = 1817
brazil = 1822
bolivia = 1825
(labeled = gained independence)

Wars and Revolutions in the Atlantic World, 1750–1830 **Name:** Natalie **Date:** ?/18/21

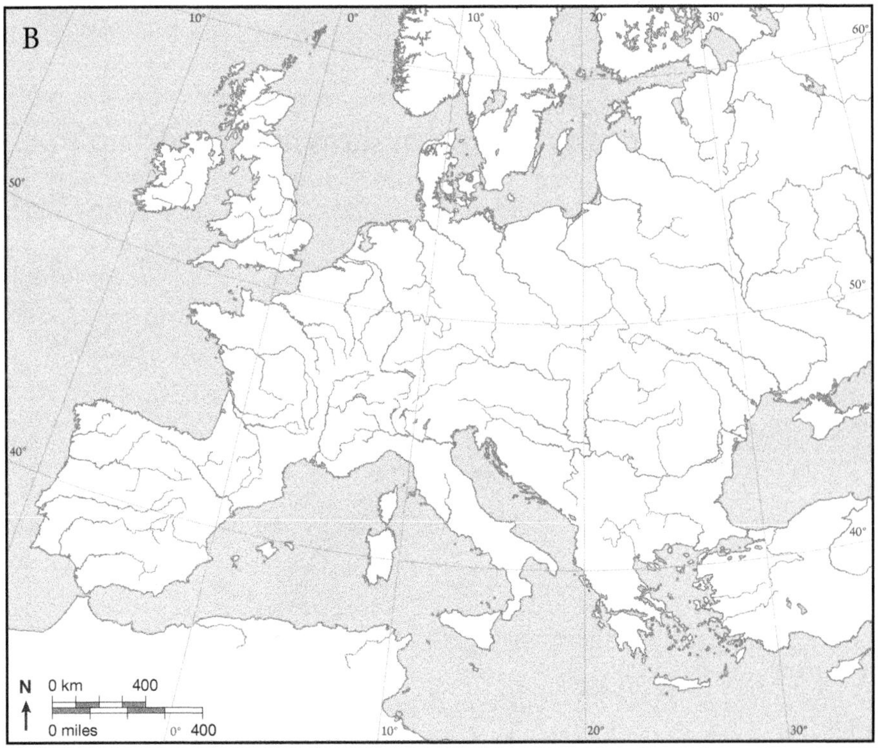
B
10°
0°
10°
20°
30°
60°
50°
50°
40°
40°
N
0 km
400
0 miles
400
0°
10°
20°
30°

The Industrializing World and Global Migrations, c. 1830–1914

* * *

1. Label and shade in red those countries that were highly industrialized by 1900.

2. Label and shade in orange those countries that were industrializing by 1900.

3. Draw yellow arrows to show Chinese migrations, c. 1830–1914.

4. Draw green arrows to show Indian migrations, c. 1830–1914.

5. Draw blue arrows to show migrations from western Europe, southern Europe, and northern Europe, c. 1850–1914.

6. Draw brown arrows to show migrations from eastern Europe and Russia, c. 1880–1914.

7. Draw a purple arrow to show Lebanese migrations, c. 1860–1914.

8. Draw black arrows to show African slave migrations up to c. 1860.

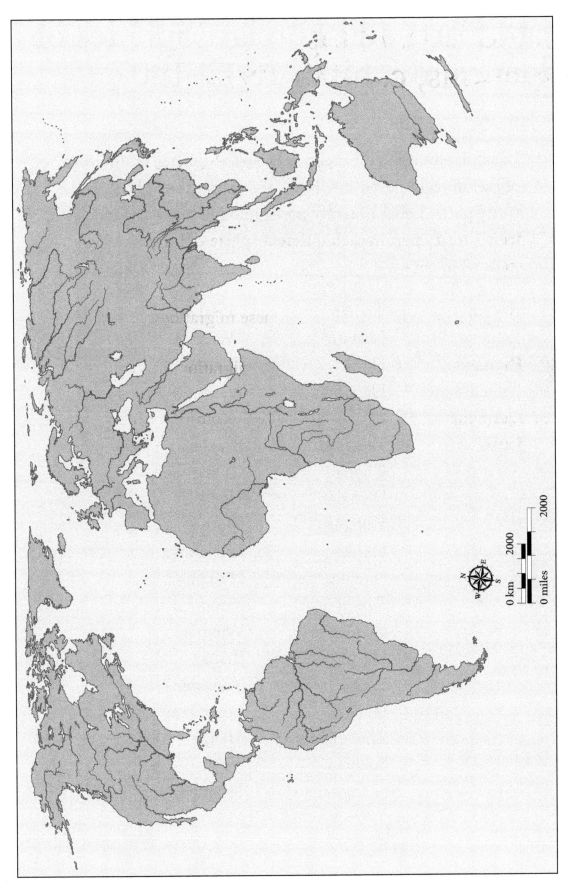

**The Industrializing World and
Global Migrations, c. 1830–1914**

Name: _____   Date: _____

Treaty Ports and Foreign Spheres of Influence in China, 1842–1907

* * *

1. Use different colored pencils to show the spheres of influence of each foreign power in China. The list on the right is all the treaty ports. Label 10 treaty ports, making sure to include at least 1 treaty port in each different sphere of influence.

Foreign powers:
Britain
France
Portugal
United States
Germany
Japan

Treaty ports:

Tianjin	Ningbo
Lüshun	Wenzhou
Dalian	Fuzhou
Dandong	Amoy
Qingdao	Shantou
Yantai	Sanshui
Chongqing	Guangzhou
Wanxian	Hong Kong
Yichang	Macao
Hankou	Zhanjiang
Nanjing	Haikou
Shashi	Jiangmen
Changshu	Wuzhou
Jiujiang	Beihai
Wuhu	Nanning
Hangzhou	Longzhou
Zhengjiang	Mengzi
Suzhou	Simao
Shanghai	Tengchong

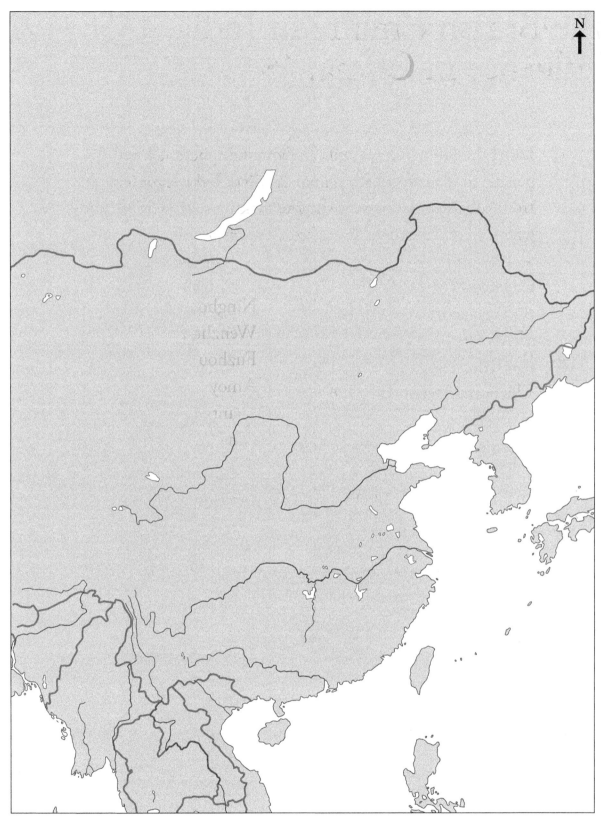

**Treaty Ports and Foreign Spheres of
Influence in China, 1842–1907**

Name: _____   Date: _____

The British Empire in India, 1858–1914

* * *

1. Label the following regions. Use three different colored
    pencils to identify which regions became British possessions
    before 1858, which were acquired by Britain after 1858, and
    which were dependent states.

    a. Ceylon
    b. Madras
    c. Travancore
    d. Mysore
    e. Hyderabad
    f. Central Provinces
    g. Bastar
    h. Orissa
    i. Chota Nagpur
    j. Gujarat
    k. Sind

    l. Rajputana
    m. Punjab
    n. Kashmir
    o. Oudh
    p. Bihar
    q. Bengal
    r. Assam
    s. Burma
    t. Lower Burma
    u. Pegu

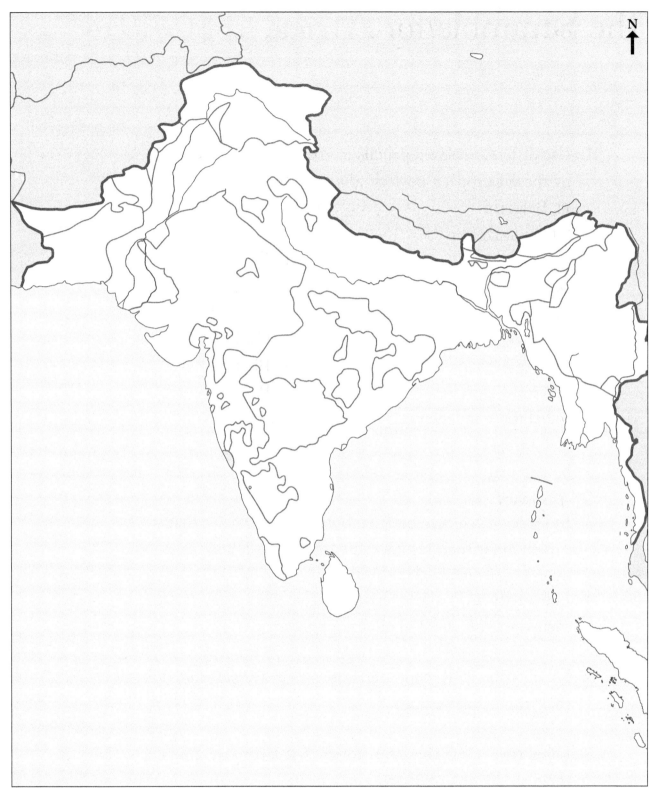

The British Empire in India, 1858–1914

Name: _____   Date: _____

The Scramble for Africa, 1880–1914*

* * *

1. Use different colored pencils to shade in the territories held
   by these European powers:
   a. Belgium
   b. Great Britain
   c. France
   d. Italy
   e. Germany
   f. Portugal
   g. Spain

2. Label these independent African states:
   a. Ethiopia
   b. Liberia

3. Indicate with a diamond symbol those territories that were
   exploited for their resources in gold, copper, and diamonds.

4. Label with a "P" those territories that were exploited for
   their resources in palm oil and/or cacao.

5. Label with an "R" those territories that were exploited for
   their rubber plantations.

6. Label with a "C" those territories that were exploited for
   their production of cotton and wheat.

*Modern day boundaries are shown

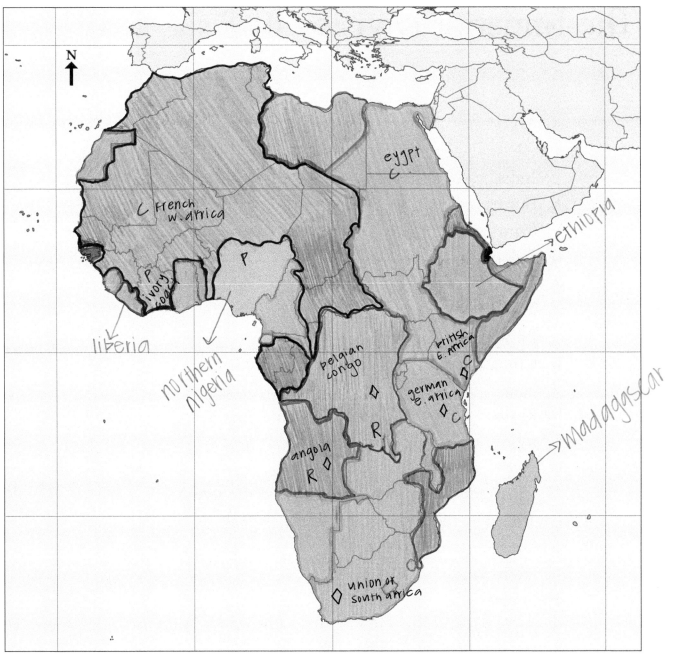

The Scramble for Africa, 1880–1914

Copyright © 2019 Oxford University Press

Name: Natalie H.   Date: 3/26/2021

🔲 = belgium   🔲 = germany   🔲 = france   🔲 = independent

🔲 = great britain   🔲 = spain

🔲 = portugal   🔲 = italy

◇ = gold, copper, diamonds

P = palm oil / cacao
R = rubber plantations
C = cotton / wheat

The Imperial Division of Asia, c. 1914

* * *

1. Label:
   a. India
   b. Burma
   c. Siam
   d. Indochina
   e. Dutch East Indies
   f. Malaysia
   g. Philippines
   h. China
   i. Japan
   j. Korea
   k. Russia
   l. Ceylon
   m. Afghanistan
   n. Formosa (Taiwan)
   o. Oman
   p. China
   q. Tibet
   r. Mongolia
   s. Iran
   t. Turkestan
   u. Siberia

2. Use different colored pencils to shade in the territory controlled by these imperial powers:
   a. Great Britain
   b. Netherlands
   c. France
   d. Japan
   e. Russia
   f. United States

3. Draw a black line to show the route of the Trans-Siberian Railway. Draw dots to mark the western and eastern terminal points of the railroad and label each terminus.

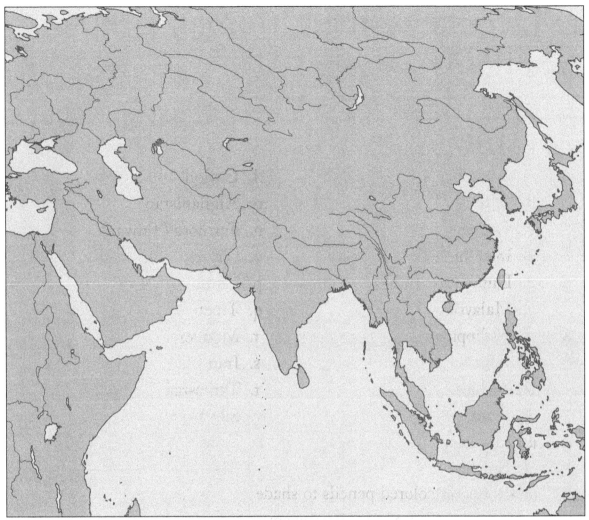

The Imperial Division of Asia, c. 1914   Name: _____   Date: _____

The Decline of the Ottoman Empire, 1683–1923

✳ ✳ ✳

1. Label:

   a. Anatolia
   b. Syria
   c. Lebanon
   d. Iraq
   e. Egypt
   f. Greece
   g. Macedonia
   h. Albania
   i. Serbia
   j. Bosnia
   k. Hungary
   l. Bulgaria
   m. Romania
   n. Transylvania
   o. Moldovia
   p. Bessarabia
   q. Podolia
   r. Crimea
   s. Crete
   t. Cyprus
   u. Palestine
   v. Cyrenaica
   w. Libya
   x. Tunis
   y. Algeria

2. Color in yellow territorial losses by 1699.

3. Color in orange losses by 1812.

4. Color in red losses by 1878.

5. Color in brown losses by 1923.

6. Color in purple Ottoman vassal states that were lost by 1912.

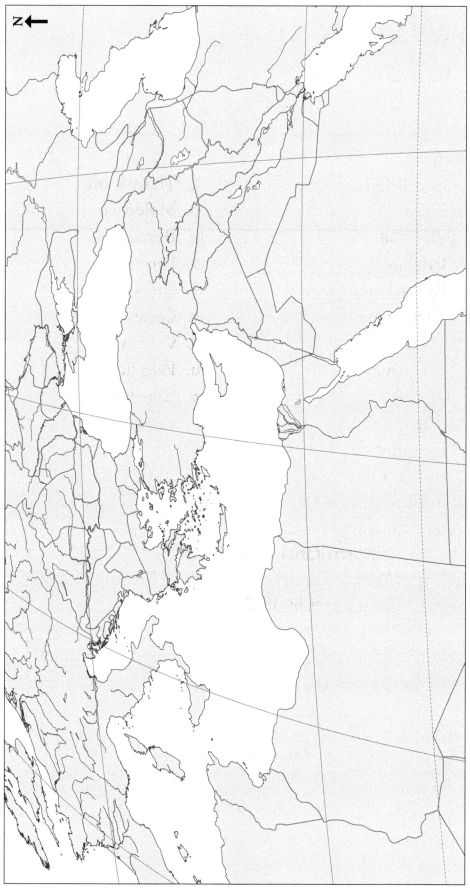

**The Decline of the
Ottoman Empire, 1683–1923**

Name: _____   Date: _____

World War I

✳ ✳ ✳

1. Label:
   a. Great Britain
   b. France
   c. Italy
   d. Germany
   e. Austria-Hungary
   f. Ottoman Empire
   g. Russia
   h. Netherlands
   i. Belgium
   j. Spain
   k. Portugal
   l. Luxembourg
   m. Bulgaria
   n. Romania
   o. Albania
   p. Serbia
   q. Greece
   r. Norway
   s. Sweden
   t. Denmark
   u. Switzerland

2. Color Allied powers green, Central powers yellow, and neutral nations pink.

3. Circle the Western Front; lightly shade in blue the area of German U-boat activity.

4. Draw red lines to show the farthest advance of the Central powers on the Western and Eastern Fronts.

5. Mark with an "X" the locations of these battles:
   a. Ypres
   b. Somme
   c. Verdun
   d. Caporetto
   e. Marne
   f. Tannenburg
   g. Gallipoli

World War I

Copyright © 2019 Oxford University Press

Name: _____ Date: _____

Women's Suffrage around the World

* * *

1. Color in red the one country that granted women full suffrage before 1914.

2. Color in pink those countries in which women were first enfranchised between 1914 and 1920.

3. Color in orange those countries in which women were first enfranchised between 1921 and 1945.

4. Color in yellow those countries in which women were first enfranchised between 1946 and 1970.

5. Color in tan those countries in which women were first enfranchised after 1971.

Women's Suffrage around the World

Name: _____   Date: _____

The Great Depression

✳ ✳ ✳

Research the decline in exports of raw materials worldwide between 1928 and 1933:

1. Color in brown those countries that experienced over an 80 percent drop in exports of raw materials.

2. Color in orange those countries that saw a decline of between 50 and 80 percent in exports of raw materials.

3. Color in yellow those countries that saw a decline of between 30 and 50 percent in exports of raw materials.

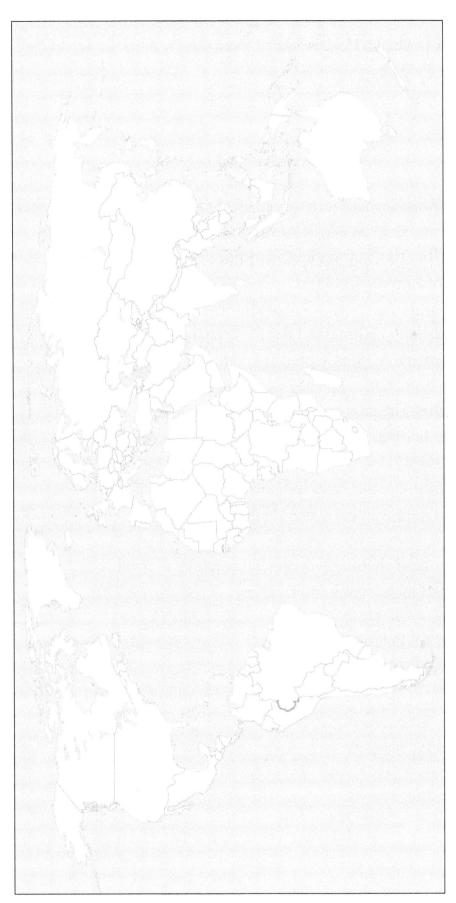

The Great Depression   Name: _____   Date: _____

The Expansion of Nazi Germany, 1933–1939

* * *

1. Outline German territory in 1933. Color in brown and label.

2. Outline the Saar region, incorporated by Germany in 1935. Color in pink and label.

3. Outline the Rhineland demilitarized zone, occupied by Germany in 1936. Color in green and label.

4. Outline the country of Austria, annexed by Germany in March 1938. Color in pink and label.

5. Outline the Sudetenland, annexed by Germany in October 1938. Color in orange and label.

6. Outline Bohemia-Moravia, annexed by Germany in March 1939. Color in red and label.

7. Outline Poland, invaded by Germany in September 1939. Color in blue and label.

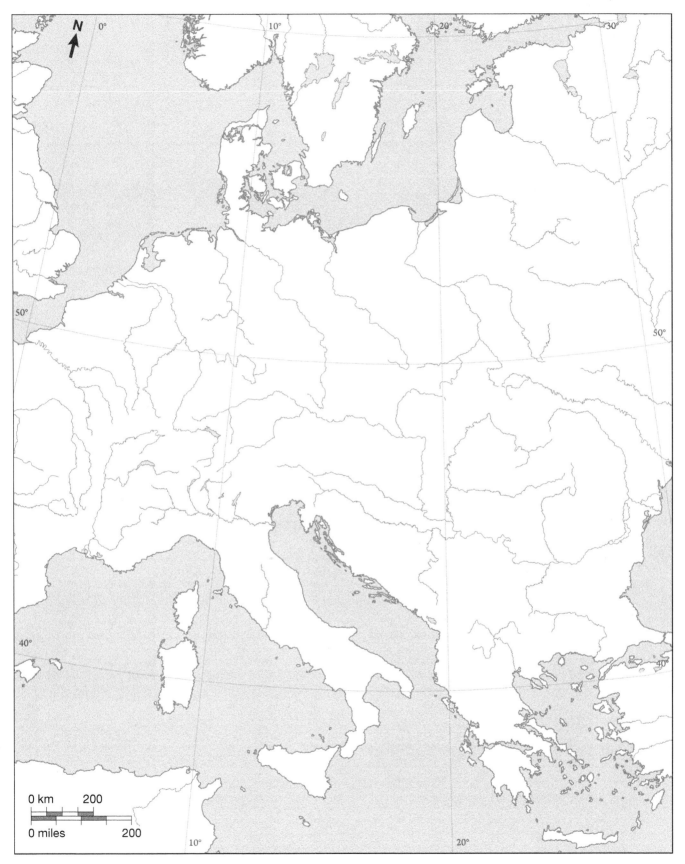

The Expansion of Nazi Germany, 1933–1939

Name: _____ Date: _____

Japanese Expansion, 1931–1942

✳ ✳ ✳

1. Label:
    a. Japan
    b. Korea
    c. Manchuria
    d. China
    e. USSR
    f. Taiwan
    g. French Indochina
    h. Philippine Islands

    i. Burma
    j. Malaya
    k. Sarawak
    l. North Borneo
    m. Dutch East Indies
    n. New Guinea
    o. Hawaiian Islands
    p. Aleutian Islands

2. Shade in red Japanese territory by 1922.

3. Shade in orange Japanese-controlled territory by 1938.

4. Shade in yellow Japanese-controlled territory by 1942.

5. Draw with a red line the farthest line of Japanese advance, July 1942.

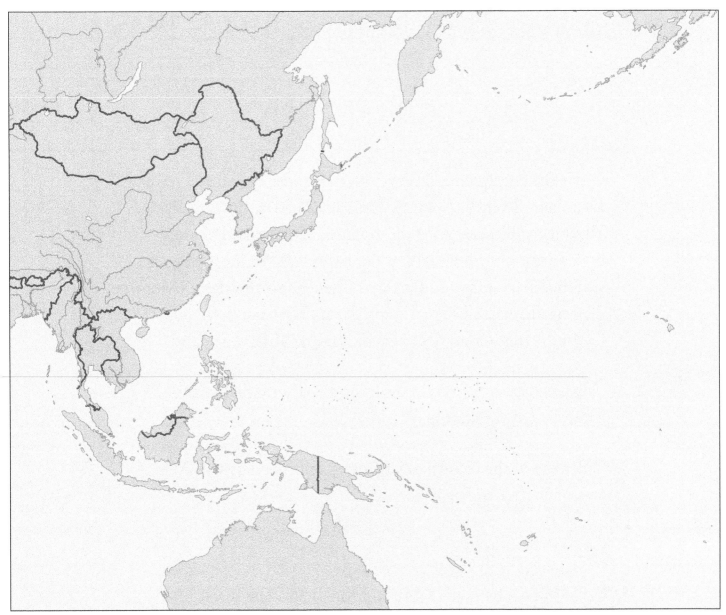

Japanese Expansion, 1931–1942

Name: _____   Date: _____

World War II in Europe, 1942–1945

* * *

1. Label:
   Great Britain, Ireland, France, Netherlands, Belgium, Germany, Denmark, Sweden, Norway, Finland, Austria, Italy, Sicily, Yugoslavia, Greece, Albania, Bulgaria, Romania, Poland, Soviet Union, Lithuania, Latvia, Estonia, Ukraine, Hungary, Czechoslovakia, Spain, Portugal, French North Africa (Morocco, Algeria, Tunisia), Libya, Egypt, Syria, Palestine, Lebanon, Cyprus, Transjordan, Iraq, Saudi Arabia, Turkey, Iceland

2. Color in brown the Axis powers and territories/colonies they controlled at the start of World War II.

3. Color in red the countries/territories controlled by the Axis powers by November 1942.

4. Color the Allies in green.

5. Color in purple the territory controlled by Vichy France.

6. Color neutral countries yellow.

7. Draw blue arrows to show Allied advances from November 1942 to May 1945.

8. Mark with a red "X" and label these major battles/landings/invasions:
   a. Kasserine Pass
   b. El Alamein
   c. Sicily
   d. Anzio
   e. Moscow
   f. Stalingrad
   g. Kursk
   h. Leningrad
   i. D-Day
   j. Battle of the Bulge
   k. Berlin

World War II in Europe, 1942–1945

Name: _____ Date: _____

World War II in the Pacific, 1942–1945

✳ ✳ ✳

1. Label:
   a. Japan
   b. China
   c. Manchuria
   d. Philippines
   e. Hawaii
   f. Australia
   g. New Guinea
   h. Dutch East Indies
   i. Burma
   j. Thailand
   k. French Indochina
   l. Aleutian Islands

2. Draw a red line around the area controlled by Japan in early 1942. Color in red major land areas it controlled.

3. Color in green areas controlled by the Allies.

4. Draw blue arrows to show Allied advances from 1942 to 1945.

5. Mark with an "X" the location of these major battles/ military engagements and label:
   a. Pearl Harbor
   b. Coral Sea
   c. Midway
   d. Guadalcanal
   e. Solomon Islands
   f. New Guinea
   g. Palau
   h. Tarawa
   i. Kwajalein
   j. Eniwetok
   k. Marianas
   l. Leyte Gulf
   m. Luzon/Manila
   n. Iwo Jima
   o. Okinawa
   p. Tokyo
   q. Hiroshima
   r. Nagasaki

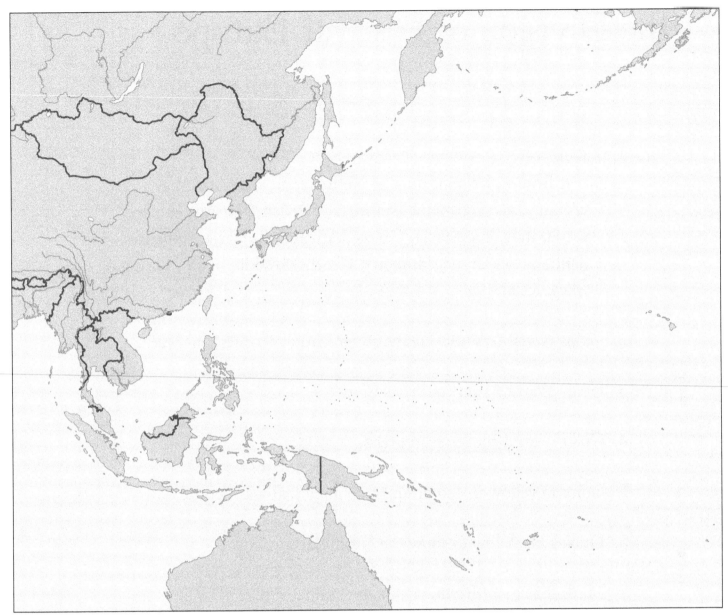

World War II in the Pacific, 1942–1945

Name: _____ Date: _____

The Division of Postwar Europe

✳ ✳ ✳

1. Label:
   Great Britain, Ireland, France, Netherlands, Belgium, West Germany, East Germany, Denmark, Sweden, Norway, Finland, Austria, Italy, Yugoslavia, Greece, Albania, Bulgaria, Romania, Poland, Soviet Union, Hungary, Czechoslovakia, Spain, Portugal, Turkey, Iceland

2. Color North Atlantic Treaty Organization countries in blue.

3. Color Warsaw Pact countries in red.

4. Color neutral countries in green.

5. Color in yellow the communist country that was neutral.

6. Draw a black line to show the "Iron Curtain."

7. Mark the city of Berlin with a dot and label it.

The Division of Postwar Europe

Copyright © 2019 Oxford University Press

Name: _____   Date: _____

Decolonization in Africa, the Middle East, and Asia

* * *

1. Shade in green those countries that achieved independence by 1950. Label each country.

2. Shade in yellow those countries that gained independence by 1956. Label each country.

3. Shade in orange those countries that gained independence by 1970. Label each country.

4. Shade in red those countries that have gained independence since 1970. Label each country.

**Decolonization in Africa,
the Middle East, and Asia**

Name: _____ Date: _____

The Cold War, 1947–1991

* * *

1. Color in blue those countries that were members of the North Atlantic Treaty Organization.

2. Color in red those countries that were members of the Warsaw Pact.

3. Color in green those countries that were members of the Non-Aligned Movement.

4. Mark with a red "X" those countries that experienced communist/leftist guerilla movements.

5. Mark with a black "X" those countries that experienced anticommunist guerilla movements.

**The Cold War,
1947–1991**

Name: _____ Date: _____

The Cuban Missile Crisis, 1962

✳ ✳ ✳

1. Label these countries:
   a. United States
   b. Cuba

2. Label these cities and places:
   a. Havana
   b. Bay of Pigs
   c. Guantanamo
   d. Key West
   e. Miami
   f. Houston
   g. Dallas
   h. New Orleans
   i. Atlanta
   j. Washington, DC
   k. New York
   l. Chicago

3. Draw a red circle to show the range of Soviet missiles based in Cuba.

4. Draw a blue circle to show the US blockade zone.

The Cuban Missile Crisis, 1962

Name: _____   Date: _____

The Oil Crisis of 1973

* * *

1. Label all the countries that were members of the Organization of the Petroleum Exporting Countries in 1973. Shade these countries brown.

2. Label all the countries that were major importers of petroleum in 1973 (over 50 million tons annually). Shade these countries red.

3. Identify and label the main combatants in the Yom Kippur War (also known as the Ramadan War or the October War).

4. Label and mark with an "X" those countries that the Organization of the Petroleum Exporting Countries embargoed in response to their support of Israel in the Yom Kippur War.

The Oil Crisis of 1973   Name: _____   Date: _____
Copyright © 2019 Oxford University Press

The Fall of Communism in Eastern Europe and the Soviet Union

* * *

1. Outline, label, and shade in yellow the former Warsaw Pact countries that broke away from the Soviet Union in 1989–1990.

2. Outline, label, and shade in pink the former Soviet republics that declared their independence in 1990–1991.

3. Shade in red and label the Russian Federation.

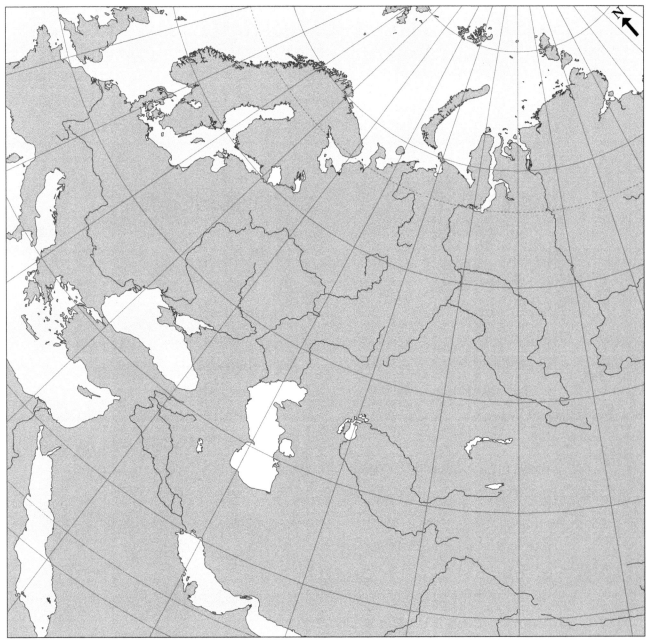

The Fall of Communism in Eastern Europe and the Soviet Union

Name: _____ Date: _____

US Military Involvement in the Middle East since 2001

✳ ✳ ✳

1. Label:
   a. Afghanistan
   b. Iran
   c. Pakistan
   d. Iraq
   e. Saudi Arabia
   f. Kuwait
   g. Syria
   h. Israel
   i. Lebanon
   j. Yemen
   k. Oman
   l. United Arab Emirates
   m. Qatar
   n. Bahrain
   o. Turkey
   p. Jordan
   q. Persian Gulf
   r. Baghdad
   s. Kurdistan
   t. Kabul

2. Draw a black arrow to show the advance of US forces in Iraq in 2003.

3. Shade in dark green those countries with a Shia majority.

4. Shade in light green those countries with a significant Shia minority (over 10 percent).

5. Draw black dots in those areas controlled by ISIS in 2014.

6. Draw red dots in those areas controlled by the Taliban in 2018.

7. Mark with an X those countries that have US military bases or station US troops.

US Military Involvement in the Middle East since 2001

Name: _____   Date: _____

A Global Economy

✳ ✳ ✳

1. Shade in blue and label those countries that are part of the North American Free Trade Agreement.

2. Shade in red and label those countries that are part of Mercosur.

3. Shade in green and label those countries that are part of the European Union.

4. Shade in yellow and label those countries that are part of the Comprehensive and Progressive Agreement for Trans-Pacific Partnership.

5. Mark with "OBOR" those countries that are part of the One Belt, One Road Initiative.

   (Several countries are members of more than one trade association.)

A Global Economy   Name: _____   Date: _____

The Threatened Environment

✳ ✳ ✳

Carbon Dioxide Emissions

1. Research the top emitters of fossil fuel carbon dioxide emissions in 2016. Label the top 10 countries and color them in black.

2. Label the next 10 countries and color them in brown.

Rainforest Destruction

1. Draw light green circles to show the extent of tropical rainforests around the world in 1900.

2. Draw dark green circles to show the extent of tropical rainforests around the world today.

Polluted Oceans

1. Research the worst oil spells in the past 50 years. Mark the locations of 10 of these spills with an "X."

The Threatened Environment

Name: _____   Date: _____

Ending Points: The Human Development Index

* * *

1. The Human Development Index scores each country according to how close it is to achieving a target standard in average lifespan of 85 years, universal access to education, and a reasonable income for all its citizens. Research the Human Development Index for 2016 and select a country that qualifies as having very high human development. Color it blue and label it. Then list the reasons why the country falls into this category.

2. Select a country that falls into the high human development category. Color it green and list the reasons why the country falls into this category.

3. Select a country that falls into the medium development category. Color it brown and list the reasons why the country falls into this category.

4. Select a country that has low human development. Color it red and list the reasons why the country falls into this category.

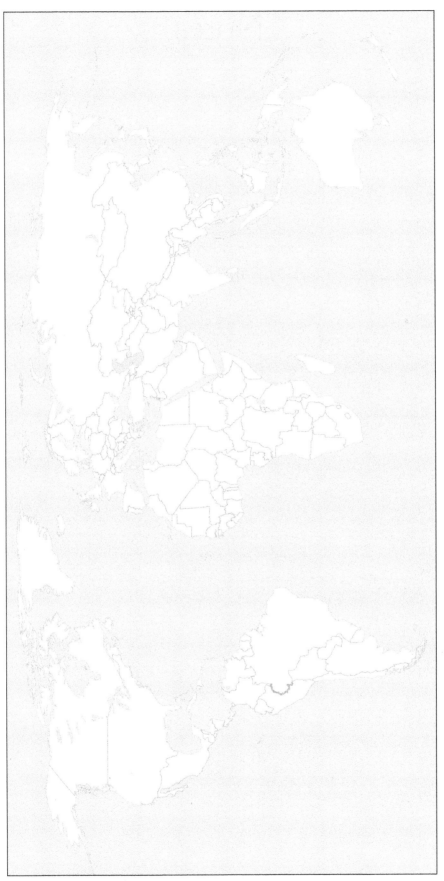

Ending Points: Name: _____ Date: _____
The Human Development Index

Notes

Notes

Notes

Notes

Notes

Notes

Notes

Notes

Notes